1

Introduction by the Vice President

Dear Mr. President,

In your State of the Union address in January, you asked me to lead an across-the-board review of America's job training programs to ensure they share a single mission: providing workers with the skills they need to secure good jobs that are ready to be filled. This report details specific actions that the Administration is taking as a result of this review and outlines further steps we can take in the future as we work to grow our economy and the American middle class.

Let's step back and consider the big picture. When we took office, our country was in the throes of the worst recession since the Great Depression. Millions of people were losing their jobs, homes, and retirement savings. Many middle-class Americans who had worked hard all their lives feared they would never recover.

To reverse the spiral, we enacted the Recovery Act, made historic investments in clean energy and infrastructure, unlocked critical lending to small businesses, and cut taxes for average American families. We rescued the iconic American auto industry, which has created over 460,000 jobs since 2009. We cut our deficit by more than half as a share of the economy, the most rapid reduction since the end of World War II. We enacted Wall Street reforms to prevent another crash on Main Street and provided millions of Americans access to affordable and secure health insurance.

Thanks to your strong leadership, and because of the grit and determination of the American people, we are growing again, and our competitive edge is sharper than ever. Businesses are hiring at historic rates, with 52 consecutive months of net private sector job growth. Manufacturing is back, with 668,000 new jobs in the past 52 months. Exports have increased to record-breaking levels for four straight years, reaching $2.3 trillion in 2013. We have the world's most skilled and productive workers, the strongest intellectual property laws, the most affordable and reliable energy supply, and the finest research institutions.

The world has taken notice. According to A.T. Kearney's annual survey of global business leaders, in 2013 the United States overtook China, India, and Brazil to be the world's single most attractive location for foreign investment, for the first time since 2001. In 2014, the United States was again named number one, this time by the widest margin ever recorded. In every sector, from heavy industry to advanced manufacturing to energy to information services, America is rated the best.

But as the United States becomes an ever-more attractive place to invest and expand operations, how will employers find the skilled workers they need to compete? The job-driven training agenda I present to you today is aimed at widening this pipeline. It will create new jobs and career pathways to meaningful, satisfying, and well-paying work – all by tapping the full potential of our country's greatest natural asset: the American people.

Getting middle-class Americans back on a road to success is a commitment we've shared since we took office. It's not just about economics. Our middle class is the reason we've been so resilient, so stable, and so successful as a nation. It's a basic bargain that says if you contribute to the success of a business, you get to share in the benefits, too.

Our Administration's responsibility begins with ensuring that federally funded training programs are singularly focused on getting more Americans ready to work, with marketable skills. These programs are particularly important to those hardest hit by the twists and turns of global competition, technological changes, economic isolation, or inadequate education opportunities.

We see incredible opportunities in high-growth industries like advanced manufacturing, information technology, and health care. Many dynamic companies in these sectors aren't just expanding their workforces. They are creating jobs that pay middle-class wages. Going forward, our Administration will work with leaders in these industries to promote partnerships between education and workforce institutions in order to create training programs that help Americans succeed in these growing fields. Together, we will also work to increase the number of apprenticeships, which allow individuals to earn and learn, and empower job seekers and employers with better data regarding what jobs are available and what skills are needed to fill those jobs.

In this review, I have worked closely with members of our Cabinet who share our commitment to a new skills paradigm. We have met with business leaders, community college presidents, governors and mayors, and academic experts. The consensus is clear: we must fundamentally rethink the pathways to well-paying, middle-class jobs, and open those pathways to all Americans.

Many businesses, community colleges, and state and local training programs – often funded with federal dollars – have found ways to successfully prepare Americans for these jobs. We must expand on these successful efforts and ensure that our entire system is learning from them. Some training programs aren't working well enough, and we're taking aggressive action to focus them on partnerships that train for in-demand skills and that match into in-demand jobs.

We applaud the recent passage of the Workforce Innovation and Opportunity Act, the first significant legislative reform of the nation's job training system in many years. The bill is consistent with the key job-driven elements in this report, and the overwhelming bipartisan support it received in Congress should send a strong signal. More needs to be done, and we welcome further engagement with Congress to enact other reforms that require legislative action.

The mission here is very simple, and it goes back to the central economic vision that has guided us since our first day in office: building a strong and thriving middle class. Now that we have recovered from the Great Recession, we must expand opportunity to the people who need it most: the working men and women who represent the backbone of the world's most dynamic and thriving economy.

It was my pleasure to lead this effort and to work with the dedicated staff across the Administration.

Sincerely,

Joe Biden
Vice President of the United States

1 Ready to Work

1.1 THE 180-DAY ASSIGNMENT: PRESIDENTIAL MEMORANDUM ON JOB-DRIVEN TRAINING

"So tonight, I've asked Vice President Biden to lead an across-the-board reform of America's training programs to make sure they have one mission: train Americans with the skills employers need, and match them to good jobs that need to be filled right now. That means more on-the-job training, and more apprenticeships that set a young worker on an upward trajectory for life. It means connecting companies to community colleges that can help design training to fill their specific needs. And if Congress wants to help, you can concentrate funding on proven programs that connect more ready-to-work Americans with ready-to-be-filled jobs."

— President Obama, State of the Union, January 28th, 2014

In his 2014 State of the Union address, as President Obama called for "a year of action" and predicted "a breakthrough year for America" in 2014, he emphasized the vital priority of equipping Americans with the skills needed to realize the economic opportunity that a renewed American economy could provide.

Two days later, in Waukesha, Wisconsin, he signed a *Presidential Memorandum on Job-Driven Training for Workers*, assigning Vice President Biden and the Secretaries of Labor, Commerce, and Education – working closely with the National Economic Council, the Domestic Policy Council, the Council of Economic Advisers, the Office of Science and Technology Policy, and the Office of Management and Budget – to develop within 180 days an action plan to make America's workforce and training system "more job-driven, integrated and effective." The *Presidential Memorandum* called for this action plan to include "concrete steps to make federal workforce and training programs and policies more focused on imparting relevant skills with job-market value, more easily accessed by employers and job seekers, and more accountable for producing positive employment and earning outcomes for the people they serve."

Under the leadership of Vice President Biden, Secretary of Labor Tom Perez, Secretary of Commerce Penny Pritzker, and Secretary of Education Arne Duncan, the Administration engaged in an intensive review to identify, initiate, and implement actions to make federal employment and training programs and policies more job-driven and effective, consistent with existing statutory authority.

This review benefitted from the work not only of the Departments of Labor, Commerce, and Education, but also from the constructive engagement of Cabinet Secretaries and leaders of employment, training, education, and workforce development programs in the Departments of

Agriculture, Defense, Energy, Health and Human Services, Housing and Urban Development, Interior, Justice, Transportation, Veterans Affairs, the Social Security Administration, and Environmental Protection Agency, and from the expertise of the Department of the Treasury, the National Science Foundation, and the Office of Personnel Management.

The *Presidential Memorandum on Job-Driven Training for Workers* emphasized the importance of looking beyond our federal programs and agencies for answers and best practices, stating specifically that the Vice President and Secretaries

> *"....shall consult with industry, employers and employer associations, state and local leaders, economic development organizations, worker representatives, education and training providers, workforce leaders, and relevant non-profit organizations."*

Consistent with that mandate, our job-driven training review included dialogue with governors, mayors, and county officials from across the country; Congressional leaders from both parties; economists who study labor markets and job opportunity; innovative and successful workforce and training practitioners serving Americans in all walks of life; labor unions whose apprenticeship programs have shown millions of Americans a path to middle-class jobs; educators in high school career academies, community colleges and universities; and some of our country's most brilliant social entrepreneurs and technology innovators.

We engaged with employers large and small in every part of the country, business leaders across virtually all American industries, human resource executives, and hiring managers to understand what it will take for employers to fill the jobs they need today and will need tomorrow with skilled American workers, and what it would mean to their prospects for expansion and success in a global marketplace.

Job-Driven Training Review Consulted Stakeholders

Employers, CEOs, small business owners

Educational leaders at community colleges, universities, and high school CTE programs

Workforce and job training partnerships, American Job Centers, community leaders

Union apprenticeship programs and labor-management partnerships

Tech innovators and social entrepreneurs

Job seekers, workers, and students

Public servants in state and federal agencies

Academic researchers and policy experts

State and local elected officials

Members of Congress in both parties

Most importantly, we heard from Americans working hard to earn a living, to find a new job, to build a career or become an entrepreneur, to bounce back from a temporary setback, to balance work and family commitments while investing in their own skills, and to reap the rewards of their hard work.

In conversations with employers, workers, and training institutions, we heard three consistent problems:

5

1   EMPLOYERS can't find enough skilled workers to hire for in-demand jobs they must fill to grow their businesses.

2   EDUCATION AND TRAINING PROGRAMS need better information on what skills those in-demand jobs require.

3   HARD-WORKING AMERICANS, whether studying, looking for work, or wanting better career paths, often aren't sure what training to pursue and whether jobs will be waiting when they finish.

Even more striking than the challenges, however, were the common-sense solutions and game-changing opportunities that we discovered. Every problem identified in this review is already being addressed in inspiring ways somewhere in America, usually by purposeful collaboration among some mix of local employers and business associations, local and state governments, American Job Centers and workforce boards, community colleges and universities, unions and labor-management partnerships, community organizations, and social entrepreneurs.

So, even as we identify where our employment and training system falls short of what we ought to expect of it, we need to keep our eyes on the real prize. The most important result of this review will be to identify and multiply what is working best today. Our job-driven training review has therefore also recommended, initiated, and in some cases implemented changes to competitive grants and administrative actions or guidance to states. These changes are all designed to create information, incentives, and inspiration for American industry, education, philanthropy, and technology to innovate, to replicate, and to scale up solutions to enable ordinary Americans to find pathways to good jobs and careers, employers to recruit and hire skilled workers their businesses need to compete, and American communities to attract business investment and create jobs by building skilled workforces.

Fortunately, as 52 consecutive months of private sector job growth make skilled workers harder to find, American industry is getting mobilized to invest in Americans' job skills, just as global businesses are once again seeing the United States as the most attractive place in the world to invest, expand, and hire.

1.2 MAKING OUR FEDERAL EMPLOYMENT AND TRAINING PROGRAMS MORE JOB-DRIVEN

The *Presidential Memorandum on Job-Driven Training for Workers* called for an action plan within 180 days to make federal employment and training programs more job-driven. Led by Vice President Biden, federal agencies and the White House have responded to this call to action.

The actions that agencies are taking will make programs serving over 21 million Americans every year more effective and accountable for training and matching Americans into good jobs that employers need to fill. These programs serve veterans, recently laid-off workers, youth and adults lacking basic workforce skills, Americans with disabilities, those recovering from serious setbacks, and those seeking better career paths.

The effort to make our federal training programs more job-driven has been buoyed by the recent passage by overwhelming bipartisan majorities in Congress of the Workforce Innovation and Opportunity Act (WIOA), which improves business engagement, accountability, access, and alignment across programs.

Providing Leadership to Our Training System: the Job-Driven Checklist

This job-driven training review has identified what is working best today around the country to help job seekers prepare for in-demand jobs and careers: job-driven training. Working together across federal agencies providing employment and training programs, we agreed on the job-driven "checklist" below to guide administrative reforms, to ensure that what's working best becomes what all Americans can expect from federally funded employment and training programs.

Each of these checklist elements is based on evidence of what's working, summarized in _What Works in Job Training: A Synthesis of the Evidence,_ an evaluation report promised in the _Presidential Memorandum._ For example, studies randomly assigning people to job training programs with extensive employer engagement within a sector found that participants were employed at a higher rate and at higher earnings (an additional $4,500 per year after individuals completed the training) than those who went through other reemployment or training programs.[1] Similarly, the support for earn-and-learn strategies, and particularly apprenticeships, is based on strong evidence that these strategies benefit individuals and employers. A recent study found that participants in Registered Apprenticeship programs earned about $7,000 more annually by their sixth year after enrollment, and over $300,000 more over their lifetime, than a comparison group of individuals who did not participate in Registered Apprenticeships.[2] This checklist embodies evidence-based practices.

The federal government will lead by example. As a result of this review, we are using the Job-Driven Checklist as a tool to maximize the effectiveness of over 25 competitive grant programs, to direct state and local training and employment programs to become more job-driven, to make sure all federal employment and training programs are engaging employers, and to improve information on employment results so we know what's working well and what's not.

---

[1] Carol Clymer, Maureen Conway, Joshua Freely, Sheila Maguire, and Deena Schwartz, "Tuning In to Local Labor Markets: Findings From the Sectoral Employment Impact Study," _Public/Private Ventures_ (July 2010).
[2] Debbie Reed, et al., "An Effectiveness Assessment and Cost-Benefit Analysis of Registered Apprenticeship in 10 States," _Mathematic Policy Research_ (July 2012).

ENGAGING EMPLOYERS

Work up-front with employers to determine local or regional hiring needs and design training programs that are responsive to those needs. Job-driven training begins by working with employers, industry associations, and labor unions early in the process of designing education and job training programs. Training programs should coordinate with employers to make sure they train individuals with skills that have a high likelihood of leading to employment. Programs should also seek employer commitments to contribute to the program through the provision of work-based learning opportunities and/or commitments to hire program graduates.

Apprenticeship in Pennsylvania

In apprenticeship programs, individuals are hired and earn wages while they participate in training that leads to a higher-wage job. The MANUFACTURING 2000 (M2K) entry-level machining program, run by New Century Careers, is an apprenticeship program that recruits un/underemployed and low-income individuals and provides hands-on training developed in collaboration with industry in addition to technical math, machine theory, blueprint reading, and metrology. Skills are verified through National Institute of Metals Working Skills standards and credentials. An employer expo upon completion of the program provides on-site interviewing, employment offers, and indefinite job placement assistance. Fees are paid by partner companies that hire M2K graduates help sustain the program.

EARN AND LEARN

Offer work-based learning opportunities with employers – including on-the-job training, internships and pre-apprenticeships and Registered Apprenticeships – as training paths to employment. While classroom time can be important, individuals can quickly learn skills where hands-on experience in a work environment is integrated with classroom learning. Job-driven training programs aim to include work-based learning opportunities that best suit their participants. These can include paid internships, pre-apprenticeships, Registered Apprenticeships, and on-the-job training.

SMART CHOICES

Make better use of data to drive accountability, inform what programs are offered and what is taught, and offer user-friendly information for job seekers to choose programs and pathways that work for them and are likely to result in jobs. In order to determine what skills should be taught and to guide job seekers as they choose what to study and where to apply for jobs, programs should make better use of data to understand current and projected local, regional, state, and national labor markets. These data may include information on the number and types of jobs available; projected regional job growth; and specific job characteristics, skills requirements, and career opportunities. These data should be publicly available and easily accessible by job seekers.

MEASUREMENT MATTERS
Measure and evaluate employment and earnings outcomes. Knowing the results of individual job-driven training programs – how many people are hired and stay employed, and how much they earn – is essential both for job seekers to choose training wisely and for programs to continuously improve results. Agencies should measure outcomes, disaggregate the data to be sure all participants are well served, evaluate programs, and inform participants and employers of the results.

Measurement Matters—Report Cards in New Jersey

New Jersey has a "consumer report card" website called New Jersey Training Opportunities that provides information on occupational training programs in the state. A results section displays information about former program participants. It shows employment rates, retention rates, and average earnings at six months, one year, and two years after graduation. New Jersey's state laws require training programs at for-profit, public two-year, and some public four-year schools that receive state or federal workforce funding to submit records to the state for all of their students, and recently required for-profit schools to submit student records and disseminate results through a state website.

STEPPING STONES
Promote a seamless progression from one educational stepping stone to another, and across work-based training and education, so individuals' efforts result in progress. Individuals should have the opportunity to progress in their careers by obtaining new training and credentials. Job-driven training programs should make it easy for individuals to transition from one post-secondary program to another, including Registered Apprenticeship and occupational training programs, and from basic education programs into post-secondary programs.

Virginia Peninsula Career Pathways

The Virginia Peninsula Career Pathways initiative is meeting manufacturers' workforce needs by engaging a consortium of 14 major employers, along with the local workforce investment board, labor unions, community colleges, and six school districts, among other partners. Based on in-depth interviews with employers, the initiative developed 11 career pathway profiles representing more than 11,000 jobs in advanced and precision manufacturing technologies on the Virginia Peninsula, and documenting necessary educational levels, credentials, and work experience requirements. The initiative takes workers where they are and helps them progress from essential skills and basic education to classroom and on-the-job training resulting in credentials and leading to employment and continual on-the-job skills upgrades and advancement, including through Registered Apprenticeships.

OPENING DOORS
Break down barriers to accessing job-driven training and hiring for any American who is willing and able to work, including access to job supports and relevant guidance. In order for training programs to work, they need to be accessible for the people who need them most. Job-driven training programs should provide access to needed supportive services such as transportation, child care, and financial and benefits counseling. Programs also should provide accommodations for persons with disabilities (including supported employment services where needed) in order to allow all individuals to benefit from these opportunities.

REGIONAL PARTNERSHIPS
Create regional collaborations among American Job Centers, education institutions, labor, and non-profits. In addition to working with employers, job-driven training programs should work with a variety of partners including Workforce Investment Boards and the American Job Centers they oversee, higher education institutions, labor organizations, philanthropic organizations, state and local human service agencies, vocational rehabilitation agencies, Medicaid agencies, centers for independent living, supported employment providers, community- and faith-based organizations, and other non-profit organizations. These partners can provide a network of employment, training and related services that help individuals overcome barriers to becoming and staying employed and serve many vulnerable populations that should be incorporated into job-driven training programs.

Encouraging Job-Driven Training Innovation to Learn Faster and Scale What Works Faster

As we spread the best of what's working throughout our training system, we also need to use our federal programs to innovate, pilot, and test promising new approaches to job-driven training. *What Works in Job Training* also identifies where we need to learn more. Major priorities include a focus on two populations where research has failed to produce evidence on effective job strategies: disconnected youth and lower-skilled individuals with various barriers to employment. In this job-driven training review, several agencies have identified opportunities to use program flexibilities to test promising models that, with evidence of effectiveness, can be scaled throughout the system.

Job-driven education and training programs should increase their focus on earning credentials based on demonstrated skills rather than simply time spent in a classroom. Higher education is strongly associated with higher earnings, but most adults in America are not in a position to attend classes full-time for years. Finding ways to finance self-paced "competency-based" education or training with Pell grants or student loans would expand and validate these more flexible programs, opening up new opportunities to upskill over 25 million low-wage workers, rapidly retool over 30 million Americans with "some college" but no degree into high demand technical or professional jobs, let millions of veterans earn educational credit for all they have learned in our nation's service, and enable millions of parents who take time off to raise children to re-enter the workforce with fresh credentials without starting over.[3] The ED will announce four new experimental sites ("X-sites") in which competency-based education models and assessments of prior learning can be tested with student financial aid.

Encouraging Collaboration within the Federal Training Programs and within States

We heard consistently from governors, mayors, state and local workforce leaders, and employers that they are frustrated at how difficult it can be to integrate the dollars from different federal programs to achieve a unified set of goals for their workforce. Some of these barriers are created by legislation, but many can be broken down administratively or with common information and "myth

---

[3] "Educational Attainment in the United States," *United States Census Bureau* (2013).

busting." We have to do better, and we can. First, we are working to encourage and facilitate collaboration at the state and local level. States have a great deal of influence in whether the programs in the state are job-driven. Governors and state workforce boards can set industry priority areas based on labor market demand. States often devote funding to attract businesses to their state and make different decisions about how training programs should support those economic development goals and what level of investment in their workers is expected of businesses. States also have discretion in aligning their job training systems.

Our Administration must set an example. We are working at an unprecedented level to align resources, activities, and strategies to bust silos and develop a job-driven workforce system across federal programs.

In the course of this review, federal agencies worked together to break down silos, create solutions together, share successes, and help each other to improve outcomes for the individuals they serve.

> The Departments of Labor and Commerce are working together to better align job training into economic development and to make the business case for apprenticeship to employers.

> The Departments of Labor and Agriculture are partnering to identify promising collaborations between the Supplemental Nutrition Assistance Program (SNAP) Employment & Training program and the broader workforce system that can be disseminated widely.

> The Department of Housing and Urban Development teamed up with the Department of Labor to provide guidance and tools for partnerships between public housing authorities and employer-led Workforce Investment Boards to generate more job opportunities for HUD-assisted residents.

> Ten federal agencies are working together to help people with disabilities prepare to qualify for the array of jobs offered by federal contractors; connect federal contractors with jobs to qualified job seekers with disabilities; and provide federal contractors with the tools and resources they need to recruit, retain, and promote people with disabilities.

This "silo busting" work will continue, spreading job-driven training best practices more rapidly among federal agencies.

1.3 THE BUSINESS CASE: MOBILIZING INDUSTRY, EDUCATION, INNOVATORS AND COMMUNITIES FOR SKILLS AND JOBS

"25 to 1": The Role of Industry, Employers, and Innovators in Job-Driven Training

At their best, federal job training programs help employers to hire the workers they need and help millions of Americans to recover from their worst experiences or stretch to reach their full potential. They change lives and livelihoods.

However, some perspective is in order. Using an expansive definition, federal employment and training programs are funded at just over $17 billion in the FY 2014 federal budget. By way of comparison, in 2013, U.S. employers are estimated to have spent over $450 billion on training, overwhelmingly for their own employees.[4] This amounts to 25 times more than the federal government spends on job training.

The role employers and industry play in shaping American job training, post-secondary education, and the skills pipeline of American workers is far larger even than those numbers suggest, as employer actions such as recruitment, hiring, participation in job fairs, and partnerships with local Workforce Investment Boards determine job market "demand." Additionally, the choices of students, job seekers, and workers about where or what to study or train, where to apply for a job or internship, or even whether it's worth putting in the effort at all, are determined in large measure by what they think will matter to employers.

The active engagement of businesses and employers is vital to ensure that training and education delivers Americans the skills needed to be productive and decently rewarded in rapidly-changing industries and a globalizing economy. The Administration is working with industry and using competitive grant programs to make our entire system, not just federal programs, more job-driven. The American Apprenticeship and Trade Adjustment Assistance Community College and Career Training (TAACCCT) grants announced by President Obama and Vice President Biden at Allegheny Community College in Pennsylvania on April 16th emphasized three key strategies:

1   Expanding Apprenticeships and On-the-Job Training. Apprenticeship programs and on-the-job training opportunities allow workers to earn while learning job-relevant skills and to advance their careers.

2   Catalyzing Education-Workforce-Industry Partnerships. Partnerships among businesses, educational institutions, Workforce Investment Boards, and other stakeholders are vital to promote job-driven training. Businesses can help ensure that education and training programs are designed to teach in-demand skills and can create demand to hire the graduates of those programs.

3   Improving Job Matching by Hiring Based on Competencies and Credentials. To better match individuals with job opportunities and relevant job training, education and training institutions need to know what skills are in demand by employers and how job seekers can demonstrate those skills. Hiring based on well-defined competencies and credentials can help education and training programs offer better career guidance and develop job-driven curricula for students and help students and job seekers make smarter choices.

---

[4] Anthony P. Carnevale, Tamara Jayasundera, and Andrew R. Hanson, "Career and Technical Education: Five Ways That Pay," *Georgetown University Center on Education and the Workforce* (2012).

Learning and Earning: American Apprenticeships and On-the-Job Training

Apprenticeships are a proven path to employment and the middle class: 87 percent of apprentices are employed after completing their programs, and the average starting wage for apprenticeship graduates is over $50,000.[5] Studies from other countries show that employers reap an average return of $1.47 for every dollar they invest in apprenticeships in increased productivity and performance.[6] Unfortunately, too few American workers and employers have access to this proven training solution to prepare for better careers or meet their needs for a skilled workforce.

Since January, our review has consulted a wide variety of employers, unions, other stakeholders, and experts extensively on opportunities to expand Registered Apprenticeships. In June 2014, DOL and DOC co-hosted six industry roundtables around the country to learn from employers what it would take to expand apprenticeships in their fields and to guide the development of new capabilities at the Office of Apprenticeship to assist employers in starting or expanding apprenticeships. Employers shared strategies for expanding apprenticeships, highlighted successful models, and identified areas where further innovation is needed for apprenticeships to scale. States are innovating.

> Apprenticeship Carolina. South Carolina took a comprehensive approach to expanding apprenticeships in the state, which have grown more than seven-fold over the past few years, from fewer than 1,000 apprentices in 2007 to more than 5,000 today. By offering employers a modest $1,000 tax credit per apprentice and establishing Apprenticeship Carolina, an apprenticeships marketing and employer assistance office within the state technical college system, South Carolina has made it easier for employers to design and launch apprenticeship programs tailored to their companies' needs. Employers as diverse as CVS, Caterpillar, and Duke Energy have launched apprenticeship programs in the state.

> Piloting new models in Detroit. Similarly, to help get residents back to work and prepare them for better jobs, Michigan has piloted an apprenticeship model in Detroit with $5,000 per employer in state workforce funding to offset training costs and, through outreach to the business community and local unions, successfully places apprentices with employers looking to grow their workers' skills.[7] Of the 33 DOL competitive Job-Driven National Emergency Grants awarded in June, 20 of them funded apprenticeship programs.

In June, DOL convened six regional summits with key high-growth industry sectors to promote the apprenticeship model and to ensure future federal investments meet business needs for skilled workers. This effort culminated in a White House Summit on American Apprenticeship on July 14th, with small and large employers such as IBM, Bank of America, Blue Cross Blue Shield of South Carolina, and Oberg Industries, labor unions like IBEW and the SEIU, training providers, community colleges, and local and state workforce leaders. Together, these groups are partnering to change the face of American apprenticeships.

---

[5] "American Job Training Investments: Skills and Jobs to Build a Stronger Middle Class," *White House Fact Sheet* (April 2014).
[6] "It Pays to Hire an Apprentice: Calculating the Return on Training Investment for Skilled Trades Employers in Canada," *Canadian Apprenticeship Forum* (June 2009).
[7] "Feds Praise Detroit Model for Apprenticeship Placement," *Employment and Training Reporter* (July 2013).

Also, DOL and ED have partnered to develop an innovative model for obtaining college credit while in apprenticeship. The Registered Apprenticeship College Consortium (RACC) is a partnership among community colleges, national accreditors, employers, and major apprenticeship sponsors, making it possible for apprenticeship graduates to earn credits that will transfer to any community college in the consortium they attend. Since it was launched in April by the Vice President, 33 more colleges and systems, including four national Registered Apprenticeship sponsors with more than 500 affiliated local programs, and three statewide community college systems have applied to join the consortium.

Regional Apprenticeship Summits

Transportation	Health care	Construction	Energy	Manufacturing	Technology
Atlanta	Boston	Washington	Houston	Chicago	San Francisco
June 4th	June 6th	June 12th	June 17th	June 19th	June 27th

We are using such collaborations to expand access to apprenticeships and their proven pathways into the middle class to more Americans. Through a partnership between VA and DOL, employers now have a fast track for their veteran employees to access their GI Bill benefits for Registered Apprenticeships, helping more than 9,000 veteran apprentices receive the benefits they have earned.[8] In addition, given that women only make up 7 percent of apprentices, DOL started apprenticeship assistance centers to support employers looking to recruit more women into technical apprenticeships.[9] In partnership with its advisory board of employers, unions, and training providers, DOL's Office of Apprenticeship is working to expand pre-apprenticeships through highlighting successful programs to increase awareness of and access to apprenticeships for a greater diversity of America's workers.

Already, we are seeing results. Employers and unions ranging from Ford and UPS to the UAW have pledged to add tens of thousands more. There are now 10,000 more apprenticeships in America than there were when the President issued his call in January.[10]

Regional Partnerships of Industry, Education, and Workforce Institutions

Despite the importance employers place on their degrees in hiring criteria, higher education institutions have struggled to keep up with the skills and competencies employers need, in part because of a poor understanding of those needs. There are hundreds of successful collaborations between four-year colleges or community colleges with employers to tailor programs, but these still are more the exception than the norm. This number has grown dramatically over the course of the past few years and even in the past year. There is a movement emerging that our policies are beginning to fuel.

---

[8] "American Job Training Investments: Skills and Jobs to Build a Stronger Middle Class," *White House Fact Sheet* (April 2014).
[9] "White House Summit on American Apprenticeship," *White House Blog* (July 2014).
[10] Internal RAPIDS calculation, *U.S Department of Labor.*

Partnerships produce better results for employers and individuals alike. Job seekers who participate in training programs developed in close partnership between industry, education, and workforce have better shots at learning the specific skills that will lead to jobs.

> PG&E PowerPathway program. Through the PG&E PowerPathway program, collaboration with local community colleges and community-based training centers, the public workforce development system, unions and industry employers, PG&E has trained more than 400 students since 2008, 71 percent of whom have found employment either at PG&E or in its suppliers. These workers are more successful on the job, and 70 percent of those job seekers hired from the PowerPathway candidate pool progress into higher job classifications within one year of hire.

Partnerships with training organizations can improve the efficiency and effectiveness with which employers can fill job openings and meet their overall hiring needs. Such industry training partnerships work best when multiple employers participate, define the skills, and hire, making the programs more portable.

DOL's Trade Adjustment Assistance Community College and Career Training (TAACCCT) competitive grant program was designed to organize exactly these kinds of partnerships. Over the last three years, TAACCCT has supported community colleges in creating partnerships with employers and industry to develop training programs that meet needs for in-demand jobs. Since 2011, 185 community college partnerships, representing more than 800 community colleges nationwide, have been awarded grants of $2.5 to $20.5 million totaling approximately $ 1.5 billion in federal funds.[11]

In April, the President and Vice President announced the availability of the final round of the TAACCCT grants, making about $450 million available to community colleges to create training programs that will help people become employed in high-growth fields. Employer engagement has been a key feature of all rounds, and in this last round, community colleges were incentivized to partner with national and/or regional industry associations and employer-led Workforce Investment Boards that commit to help design and implement job training programs based on industry-recognized credentials that can be replicated with other education and training institutions across the country where industry also needs to hire workers with those skills. They were also incentivized to work across community colleges in the state and other education and training institutions to create state career pathways systems that create on-ramps and off-ramps for workers and clear transfer routes from one degree program to another.

But career readiness needs to start early. Too few of America's students are exposed to learning that links their studies in school to future college and career pathways. To spur the emergence of successful partnerships targeting career readiness for young people, in April the President announced the winners of DOL's Youth CareerConnect grants that provided $107 million – enough to support 31,000 students – to partnerships of local education agencies, Workforce Investment Boards, institutions of higher education, and employer partners as they redesign teaching and learning to more fully prepare youth with the knowledge, skills, and industry-relevant education needed to get on the pathway to successful career.

---

[11] *U.S. Department of Labor.*

Los Angeles Career Academies. The Los Angeles Unified School District, for example, is receiving a $7 million grant to build out new career academies in six high schools that will focus on health care, biotechnology, and other technology-related industries. The program is backed by funding from the Irvine Foundation. The United Way of Greater Los Angeles, the Los Angeles workforce investment system, and Los Angeles Chamber of Commerce will help provide work-based learning opportunities to students, including 10,000 student summer internships.

To further support such partnerships among education, workforce and industry, DOL will also promote and support regional workforce and industry partnerships that include business and industry, community colleges and training providers, labor unions, non-profits and community organizations, and philanthropy working together with the workforce system to promote economic competitiveness and create pathways to the middle class and beyond for a wide range of workers. In collaboration with DOC and tapping the expertise of other federal agencies, DOL's Center for Workforce & Industry Partnerships will promote existing partnerships, catalyze new ones, and form a common vision and approach to workforce and industry partnerships.

Job Matching: Data, Guidance, and Credentials to Empower Job seekers and Employers

Today, an unemployed worker may submit her resume for countless job openings without getting a call back to interview or feedback as to what she should do differently in the future to improve her chances. Employers, on the other hand, report an inability to find skilled workers for jobs they want to fill: according to Manpower, 39 percent of U.S. companies reported difficulty filling positions in 2013 because of a lack of skills – a substantial increase from the 14 percent of employers who reported such difficulty in 2010.[12] Improving job matching presents an opportunity to connect more job seekers to jobs that utilize their skills. It also promises benefits to employers, as the search costs of filling vacancies are high: according to one survey, the average U.S. company spends $3,500 per new hire in advertising costs and human resources staff salaries. [13] These costs can be severe. Solutions to this job matching problem would benefit employers and the American economy, cutting down job search costs, raising employee satisfaction, improving productivity and reducing costly employee turnover.

Industry-recognized credentials can grease the wheels of job matching by allowing job seekers to signal clearly to employers what skills they possess. For example, the Cisco Certifications System (CCS) is a successful example of credentials that allow individuals to demonstrate their competencies to install, maintain, and troubleshoot Cisco networking equipment at ascending levels of sophistication, in ways that thousands of employers recognize and trust. Around 700,000 U.S. workers are certified in one or more of the 45 different CCS certifications, many of which are available at no cost. A number of other software platform companies – such as Microsoft, Esri, and MongoDB – offer such certifications, and many more should do so as a business strategy to ensure that their software is used effectively by their customers.

---

[12] 2013 Talent Shortage Survey Research Results," *ManpowerGroup* (2013).
[13] Karen O'Leonard, "The Talent Acquisition Factbook 2011," *Bersin & Associates* (2011); Steven J. Davis, R. Jason Faberman, and John C. Haltiwanger, "The Establishment-Level Behavior of Vacancies and Hiring," *The Quarterly Journal of Economics* (2013).

Programs that train individuals to earn industry-recognized credentials offer job seekers a clear value proposition. For example, the mean annual wage for those with a Cisco Certified Network Associate credential, Cisco's most popular entry-level credential, is roughly $80,000, and many individuals quickly rise to network management jobs or earn cybersecurity credentials that can earn well over $100,000 per year.[14]

Hiring based on industry-recognized credentials reduces search costs and raises productivity for employers, both in having more skilled workers, and in knowing reliably what skills they can expect from those workers. While the IT field may be the most advanced, industries as diverse as manufacturing, energy, and retail are working to develop nationally-recognized credentials, including 22 business and industry associations organized into a national network by the Business Roundtable and a coalition of five philanthropic foundations.

DOL online tools and access to data on jobs and skills. Technology platforms and applications can help bridge the gaps between Americans looking for work and employers looking for workers. DOL has created several online career tools to help job seekers plan their careers, choose which jobs to apply for, and identify training and certifications needed to be successful on the job. In addition to creating tools for job seekers and career counselors, DOL has opened its data sets, made them available on data.gov, and created web services for use by states, local areas, businesses and developers. O*NET (www.onetonline.org) has detailed descriptions of the world of work for use by job seekers, workforce development and HR professionals, students, researchers and more.

Data jams with job seekers and tech innovators. The Administration is also helping to catalyze entrepreneurial development of job-matching apps and highlight successful models. Vice President Biden and the White House Office of Science and Technology Policy hosted a "Data Jam for Job Seekers" in June, bringing together dozens of technology innovators and leaders of innovative state workforce systems to mock up new apps and uses of data that can help match job seekers and employers, and to help current workers find paths to be trained for better jobs and careers. Those teams are working now to create prototypes of these apps that will be demonstrated and launched at a White House "Datapalooza for Job Seekers" later this fall.

Open data for job-driven training. The President's open data initiatives continue to release valuable data sets on jobs and skills, making them freely available online. These data can be used by private sector innovators and governments alike to create better tools to match job seekers to available jobs and training and to help policy-makers make data driven decisions on how best to allocate resources.

---

[14] "2013 IT Skills & Salary Report: A Comprehensive Survey from Global Knowledge and Windows IT Pro," *Global Knowledge Training* (2013).

1.4 THE OPPORTUNITY AHEAD: A CALL TO ACTION FOR AMERICAN SKILLS AND JOBS

Applying the Job-Driven Checklist systematically across all federal employment and training programs will allow those programs to focus scarce federal dollars on promising and proven strategies for getting people back to work. Federal employment and training programs will use them to guide their programs' priorities and operations to the extent feasible within the law and the programs' missions through competitive grants and other administrative actions.

These competitive grants and administrative actions will incentivize investments by employers in apprenticeships or on-the-job training, industry-education partnerships, and industry-driven credentials and job matching. Industry investment and employer hiring based on the three strategies described below multiplies the impact of federal training investments and focuses individual choices and training program design on in-demand jobs, expanding opportunities for all American workers. We've seen what can be accomplished when we come together. Over the past three years, the Joining Forces Initiative led by First Lady Michelle Obama and Dr. Jill Biden has garnered efforts from employers resulting in more than 540,000 jobs and numerous more commitments from iconic companies and large and small businesses to train and create stable employment for veterans and military families, and launched an online tool created by VA and DOL for employers and veterans seeking jobs featuring a skills translator, resume builder and job openings to help train and match veterans into good jobs.

> *Where can job-driven training strategies change the trajectory of economic opportunity? Where can American employers, workers, families, communities, and taxpayers achieve the highest return together by proven and innovative job-driven approaches applied in focused ways?*

This report recommends three opportunities for a call to action:

1   Fielding a Full Team. Bringing 3 million ready-to-work Americans back into jobs after being unemployed for more than six months

2   Upskilling America. Helping 24 million low-wage, lower-skill, hard-working Americans to upskill themselves into better jobs

3   Tech Workforce. Diversifying the ways that Americans of any age, in any part of the country, and from any background can be trained for half a million jobs unfilled today in IT occupations, and hundreds of thousands more that need to be filled soon

Fielding a Full Team: Getting Long-Term Unemployed Americans Back to Work

Today, 3.1 million long-term unemployed Americans – many with extensive work histories – struggle to find work in jobs that use their skills.[15] Those Americans are ready to work, now or soon – they just need to be matched to jobs fitting their skills and sometimes given targeted training to fill the gaps.

---

[15] *Bureau of Labor Statistics* (2014).

As the economy improves, it is critical that hard-hit Americans with skills, experience, and a desire to work have the opportunity to get back to work. A complex labor market can make it difficult for individuals to find the right pathways, even if they possess needed skills. Formal education requirements for jobs and employer hiring screens based on factors other than skills for the job can make it harder for people to get jobs. Job seekers can fall through the cracks of a confusing process.

At a January summit at the White House, the President called attention to the fact that the long-term unemployed risk being left behind. Since the summit, the number of long-term unemployed has declined by 500,000, accounting for more than 70 percent of the overall drop in unemployment.[16] Notably, the long-term unemployment rate fell faster over the last six months than it did over the previous six months.

Despite this progress, however, the long-term unemployment rate remains well above its 2001 to 2007 average: 3.1 million Americans are long-term unemployed today, making up 32.8 percent of all the unemployed.[17] Studies show that long-term unemployed job seekers are only half as likely to be considered for hiring, even though their education and experience levels match those of other job seekers. A recent study by Evolv found their job performance once hired to be equal that of other hires.[18] The White House has continued this focus, announced by the President in January.

Long-Term Unemployment Playbooks Following up on the White House Best Practices for Hiring and Recruiting the Long-term Unemployed. As part of their commitment to enhance employment opportunities among American workers and address the challenges the long-term unemployed typically face in finding employment, Deloitte and the Rockefeller Foundation are working together to create playbooks that can be used by employers and long-term unemployed job seekers to return a greater number of job seekers to the workforce. The employer playbook will provide tactical tools to help employers operationalize the Best Practices and tap into the full potential of the long-term unemployed population.

Many employers are already making progress in reforming their recruiting and hiring practices to help get the long term unemployed back to work. Chapter 3 highlights a few particularly promising examples of progress from Aetna, MetLife, and Frontier Communications.

Demand-Driven Training Guide to Expand and Improve Regional Partnerships. Skills for Chicagoland's Future, with support from the Aspen Institute's Skills for America's Future, has developed a guide about how to make reemployment and training programs more demand-driven. The guide is hosted at SCFplaybook.com. Skills for Chicagoland's Future has used this model to hire almost 1,000 people since launching in 2012, and 70 percent of those individuals have been long-term unemployed, showing how a demand-driven model can be effective at both meeting business needs and helping disadvantaged groups.

---

[16] *Bureau of Labor Statistics* (2014).
[17] *Bureau of Labor Statistics* (2014).
[18] Aki Ito, "Long-Term Unemployed Make for Just as Strong Hires: Study," *Bloomberg* (April 2014).

Competitive Grants to Support the Long-Term Unemployed. Efforts by outside partners to scale successful practices will improve regional partnerships and build on the increased work to train the long-term unemployed catalyzed by DOL's grants. As announced in January, DOL will award 25-30 grants in October to replicate innovative partnerships among employers and non-profits in communities across the country to prepare and place the long-term unemployed into good jobs. In June, DOL awarded $155 million to 34 states to expand promising public-private partnerships that serve long-term unemployed dislocated workers. For example, Nevada is partnering with the WorkPlace to implement the Platform to Employment program targeted at long-term unemployed jobseekers in the Las Vegas and Reno metropolitan areas.

Ensuring Federal Policies Support Hiring of the Long-Term Unemployed. The President used his executive authority to sign a Presidential Memorandum to make sure that individuals who are unemployed or have faced financial difficulties through no fault of their own receive fair treatment and consideration for employment by federal agencies.

Upskilling America: From Dead-End Jobs to Apprenticeships and Middle-Class Career Paths

There should be no dead-end jobs in America. A mom working 40 hours per week at $11 dollars per hour with no path to advancement should not have to find a second job for 20 more hours to support her family. Instead of a second job, why can't she use those extra hours to learn to do a $20 an hour job? Low-wage, entry-level jobs should be stepping stones to robust career pathways into the middle class. Whether through Registered Apprenticeships or other forms of on-the-job training, every American worker who starts in a low-wage job should have the opportunity to gain the foundational and functional job skills needed to earn more and progress as they learn and contribute more.

For example, approximately 24 million working Americans have low literacy skills, and nearly double that number struggle with numeracy.[19] There are emerging career ladders for entry-level workers who have access to the right educational content and receive some on the job training. For example, this Burning Glass Technologies analysis shows upward opportunities for Retail Sales Associates and for Retail Supervisors based on common transitions observed in the job market.[20] Retail Supervisors develop a diverse skill set that includes sales and customer service, management, administration and accounting, logistics, and security. Upward pathways can leverage any of these skills.

---

[19] Internal calculations based on OECD, *Program for the International Assessment of Adult Competencies* (2013).
[20] Methodology: Transition pathways are based on the frequency of career transitions observed in millions of resumes and analysis of skill requirements in Burning Glass's proprietary database of >100M online job postings. Wage data reflect the median hourly wage for the related SOC code.

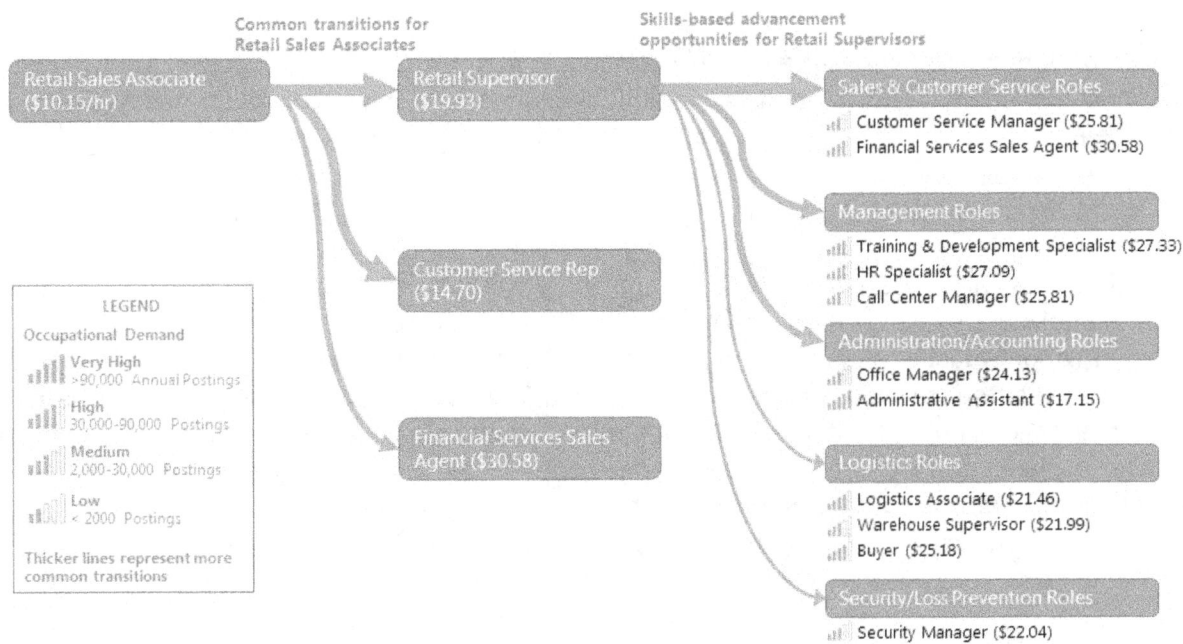

Providing opportunities in industries such as health care, retail, and hospitality, where lower-skilled and limited-English-proficient workers are concentrated, to develop their skills and enable them to access pathways for advancement to better jobs and careers would be good for employers and good for American workers. Such opportunities could include well-structured apprenticeships and career pathway programs to "upskill" low-wage employees into higher-skilled jobs with higher earnings, greater investment by employers in training of entry-level workers into higher-skilled positions, and more publically available career readiness tools geared towards working adult learners.

Our Administration is taking initial steps in partnership with innovators, workers, and employers:

Launching a $25 Million Online Skills Academy. An online skills academy will leverage technology to offer open online courses of study, helping students earn credentials online through participating accredited institutions, and will expand access to curricula designed to speed the time to credit and completion. Building off the burgeoning marketplace of free and open-licensed learning resources, including content developed through the TAACCCT grant program accessible through DOL's online repository, the online skills academy will enable workers to get more education and training they need to advance their careers, particularly by developing skills in demand by employers.

Working with Unions and Labor-Management Partnerships to Expand Quality Training Programs to Provide Pathways to Middle-Class Jobs. Working with ED, over 45 unions and labor management partnerships are pledging to expand access to their training programs and share lessons of these programs with others around the country.

New Tools for Job Seekers and Personalized Career Guidance. Following the Data Jam for Job Seekers, several innovative companies have committed to building new tools to help job seekers better understand their options so they can make smarter investments of their time and resources when trying to get jobs. For example, Glassdoor has launched a new open-source map for job seekers to see where there are open jobs county-by-county across the country.

Many employers are making high-return investments in their front-line employees' skills, working with innovators and education, workforce, union, and community partners. Others can and should follow their lead.

The Tech Workforce: Creating On-ramps to Fill America's Highest-Demand Jobs

Why do hundreds of thousands of jobs in cybersecurity, network administration, web design, coding, and data analytics go unfilled daily when millions of Americans are un- or underemployed?[21] The Bureau of Labor Statistics estimates that projects that between 2012 and 2022, 1.3 million jobs will need to be filled from new jobs and replacement need for computer occupations and information systems managers, but without serious growth in the number of people with information technology (IT) skills, it is unlikely that American workers will meet that demand[22]. Businesses, individuals, and communities across the country should seize this opportunity. Workers can boost their earnings on IT employment tracks, with strong potential for upward mobility. Businesses burdened with high IT vacancy and recruiting costs, and the U.S. economy as a whole, can become more competitive.

The need to train many more people with IT skills exists nationwide and across a broad range of employers. Recent data on the IT job market shows that Pennsylvania, Illinois, Oklahoma, and Alabama had the highest demand for IT workers relative to the installed IT talent pool.[23] And they aren't only for those with four-year or advanced degrees; some require IT skills that can be taught in less than a year.

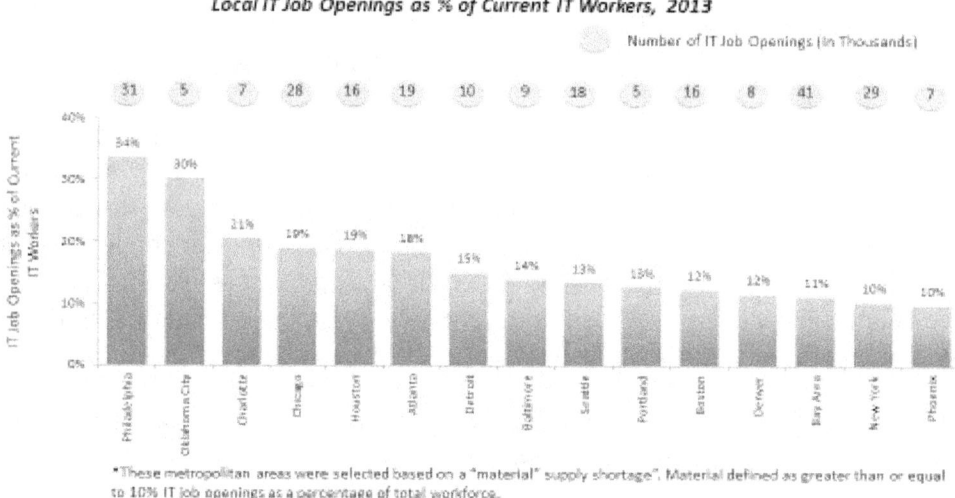

15 U.S. Cities with greater than 10% more Employer IT Job Demand than IT Worker Supply
Local IT Job Openings as % of Current IT Workers, 2013

*These metropolitan areas were selected based on a "material" supply shortage". Material defined as greater than or equal to 10% IT job openings as a percentage of total workforce.
*Metropolitan areas, including cities and surrounding suburbs
SOURCE: CEB

---

21 CEB TalentNeuron

22 C. Brett Lockard and Michael Wolf, "Occupational employment projections to 2020," *Bureau of Labor Statistics* (January 2012).

23 CEB TalentNeuron research and analysis, crawling of public profiles, skill predictor algorithms, CEB TalentNeuron Skill Taxonomy & SME Interviews. CEB, 2013.Unpublished

Closing the gap between the growing demand and the supply of IT-skilled workers cannot be achieved through any single program, initiative, or degree. That being said, preparing Americans to join the tech workforce may be more straightforward and solvable than many other challenges.

First, in IT, a number of employers are recruiting, screening, hiring using "competency-based" credentials—those that are based on what someone can do regardless of where they learned how to do it or how much time it took them.[24] These practices shape Americans' decisions about where and what to study, and training providers choices about what skills to teach. Second, new models of "accelerated training"—coding bootcamps, MOOCs, modernized apprenticeships—are letting workers move at their own pace to acquire skills tightly linked to employment and ultimately resulting in credentials that employers trust. Finally, regional partnerships that span the private and public sectors, in fields such as cyber, have seen success in improving the alignment between training and work and easing the education to employment journey for workers.

We should work to emulate the successes that, on a smaller scale, communities have achieved in the cybersecurity skill area, for example. Together the Administration alongside employers, mayors, local and regional education, training, and workforce institutions and others, could seize this opportunity to make a substantial difference in employment and wage growth nation-wide.
To begin taking advantage of the opportunity to close this gap between IT job needs and workers ready to fill them, our Administration is taking initial steps in partnership with the private sector:

Expanding Innovative Coding Bootcamps. Three cities - Kansas City, Missouri; Louisville, Kentucky; and Minneapolis, Minnesota - together with the Wadhwani Foundation are creating new public-private partnerships, working closely with local IT employers and city leaders to attract coding bootcamps. Each will quantify employer demand for IT positions and specific skills necessary to fill those jobs, and have identified funding immediately available to provide tuition support. Wadhwani will provide support to document and evaluate these efforts as they move forward.

VA Accelerated Learning Competition. To ensure that Veterans can take full advantage of innovative learning models, VA will sponsor a $10 million competition to identify leading practices among alternative learning models, and evaluate the employment outcomes of accelerated learning programs (ALPs) for post 9/11 Veterans. The competition will be a multi-staged event leading to direct funding of Veteran participation in IT centric ALPs, including coding bootcamps. This two-year demonstration project will start in FY 2015, with the help of funding through the VA Center for Innovation, and has the potential to scale to other communities based on demonstrated outcomes and the availability of resources.

National Initiative for Cybersecurity Education (NICE) to increase access to Cyber Education and Training. NICE, which is designed to improve cybersecurity education from K-12 to postgraduate schools in the United States, is developing a plan to expand pathways to cyber skills and jobs by expanding the list of DHS- and NSA-certified high-quality cyber training programs, particularly in community colleges.

---

[24] "Software Is Everywhere: Growth in Software Jobs," *Burning Glass Technologies* (July 2013). Job growth estimates based on online job posting growth proxy.

1.5 READY TO WORK ECONOMIES: A JOB-DRIVEN TRAINING AGENDA FOR AMERICAN COMMUNITIES

Regional approaches that bring together diverse institutions across communities – employers, government, training organizations, economic development agencies, labor, and others – have proven highly effective at getting Americans back to and moving up in work and simultaneously improving local economies. These strategies allow states and regions to hone in on the critical workforce needs and opportunities in their local areas, engage industry and other partners across traditional boundaries, and coordinate activities across workforce, economic development, and education within states.

To train many more Americans with the skills employers need and to match them to good jobs that need to be filled right now, we must replicate regional beacons of success, moving beyond single-case partnerships to industry-wide, systemic change. Two challenges exist:

> Communities don't have enough access to information and guidance. We are now armed with good information about what works and an increasing number of regions that are ready and willing to replicate and tailor these approaches to their local economies. But a dearth of investment in labor market information; technical assistance; and coordination among education, workforce, and economic development agencies limits the ability of regions to change their systems so that small businesses who employ most workers can leverage an infrastructure they don't have the capacity to build themselves. Doing a better job of supporting regions with ongoing streams of up-to-date, granular information on job and skill demand locally will give them the flexibility to undertake innovative, integrated approaches and achieve better results, and providing additional funding to replicate and scale proven approaches.

> There simply aren't enough resources for individuals to get the career guidance that would lead them to these programs or the training even once local employers have come together and created programs that work. Each year millions of workers are displaced from their jobs. Many workers would benefit from reemployment and training services to help them get back to work, but DOL has less funds for displaced workers today in real terms than it did in the late 1990s, when the unemployment rate was lower than 4 percent. Due to budget constraints, only 15 percent of participants in the largest federal training program for dislocated workers receive training. The Workforce Innovation and Opportunity Act has authorized an increase in annual funding levels for DOL's WIA Youth, Adult and Dislocated Worker programs. If appropriated by Congress, these funds would allow broader access to job-driven training locally.

For the lucky few, access to these resources can be life changing. One of the participants at the White House long-term unemployment event was a single mom named Danielle. Danielle ended up homeless after losing her job during the Great Recession. Danielle's life was changed because she saw a flyer in an unemployment insurance office for a manufacturing training program. She was able to get funding for that training at a local manufacturing training program and assistance with transportation to and from class. Upon graduating from the training program, she was hired as a machine operator making $18.20 per hour. Since she started, she has received a couple of wage increases, and today she makes $20.25 per hour.

In a system with more resources, more people would see flyers, or more likely, personalized recommendations via an electronic tool. Once they received good recommendations for training, they would have the assistance needed to help them complete the program. The training programs themselves need to be created in the context of regional economies, but those programs also need resources to help people. The program that helped Danielle get a job is a small organization with strong connections to local manufacturers. It's a regional solution, but the training she got was funded by the Workforce Investment Act and the transportation dollars came from Temporary Assistance for Needy Families.

The President has proposed significant increases in employment and training investments that would both help regions collaborate to create effective programs and provide funding that can be used to deliver these effective programs to more individuals.

The Community College Job-Driven Training Fund would provide $6 billion in funding over four years, increasing our current training investments significantly. This proposal would offer competitive grants to partnerships of community colleges and other public or non-profit training entities with industry and employers, to reform curricula and launch new training programs to deliver skills for in-demand jobs. Investments would focus in part on providing funding for industry-education partnerships to co-develop and disseminate common credentials and skills assessments, making it easier for workers to invest in training that will get them a job and start them on a career. $2 billion would be devoted to support President Obama's call to Congress to double the number of apprentices in America over five years. These funds would provide flexible support for comprehensive state strategies to expand apprenticeships and for innovative partnerships among employers, labor unions, training providers, and local workforce leaders. It would help align apprenticeship programs with community colleges and high schools, strengthen on-ramps and pathways into apprenticeship, and better market apprenticeships. With only 375,000 apprenticeships today – one sixth as many as Britain on a per capita basis – many more Americans could benefit from this path to skilled, well-paying work.

Making these investments would increase the capacity of local communities to develop solutions that work for local employers, meet the needs of job seekers in the region, and provide funding to help put people through newly-created or expanded programs. They would increase the number of people with access to job-driven solutions and should be priorities across political lines. We look toward working with Congress to increase resources for these important objectives.
In the meantime, we will continue to work to ensure that our current investments in employment and training are going toward job-driven approaches and mobilizing partnerships to increase the pool of resources available.

This report marks the milestone in our Administration's work to make our job training system more job-driven and improve career opportunities for job seekers and workers. It highlights the great work that is already underway by someone, somewhere across the country to make the most of these opportunities. The ideas put forward in this report are a starting point, not an end. The White House and federal agencies will seek input on other steps that can be taken to improve federal programs and identify the most innovative ideas and projects to help spread job-driven practices more broadly.

This fall, dozens of communities across the country will emerge as winners of job-driven training competitive grants, whether for workforce partnerships with businesses to train and hire the long-term unemployed, or for community college partnerships to train for in-demand jobs. At the same time, we'll call on governors and mayors, business and industry leaders, innovators and educators, unions, philanthropies and community organizations across the country to work together and commit to realizing this opportunity. We know they will answer the call, because they've asked us to make it.

America was built on hard work leading to fair reward. It was built on innovation and persistence leading to progress. As the United States economy strengthens and leads the world, and as employers in America compete to find the skilled workers they need, we can restore this basic bargain. Together we will.

2 Nuts and Bolts: Job-Driven Reform of federal Training Programs

The federal training system is made up of job training programs across 10 agencies, but more than 75 percent of funding is found in just 10 programs and over 95 percent of funding is found in four agencies. These include all the major programs that began under the Workforce Investment Act in 1998, such as Dislocated Worker funding and Adult Education for individuals with low literacy and numeracy skills. This act was a key milestone in creating today's training system. According to GAO there were approximately 163 federal workforce programs in 1995. The Workforce Investment Act was recently reauthorized as the Workforce Innovation and Opportunity Act (WIOA) and signed by the President on July 22nd, 2014. Major employment and training programs not funded by this legislation include Temporary Assistance for Needy Families (TANF), Veterans Vocational Rehabilitation and Employment, and Career and Technical Education.

Based on the best evidence available, our largest federal employment and training programs – such as the major programs authorized by the Workforce Investment Act (WIA) and the Wagner-Peyser Act – use job training and reemployment strategies that are fairly effective in raising the job prospects and earnings of Americans who use them, and the reforms initiated in this review will make them more effective.[25] For millions of Americans, particularly those hardest hit by economic setbacks (e.g., long-term unemployment) or major life disruptions (such as

Spending on Employment and Job Training Programs by Agency

4.3%
8.0%
12.5%
45.2%
29.9%

- Labor
- Health and Human Services
- Other agencies
- Education
- Veterans Affairs

those transitioning back to civilian life from military service), the direct services provided by these programs make an essential difference at critical moments.

But there remains room for improvement. Our federal training system can do a better job of making sure that all training is job-driven across large and small programs. It is also important that programs be coordinated so that individuals can get the services they need in a meaningful pathway without having to know which programs provide which services. Similarly, employers should have a common

---

[25] Sheena McConnell, Irma Perez-Johnson, and Jillian Berk, "Providing Disadvantaged Workers with Skills to Succeed in the Labor Market," *The Hamilton Project* (June 2014); also Marios Michaelides, "Are Reemployment Services Effective in Periods of High Unemployment? Experimental Evidence from the UI System" (April 2013).

point of entry to provide input and expertise to a variety of programs to make sure they are providing skills that will help people find jobs.

The Administration is taking a number of steps to make sure that federal training programs are job-driven and working collaboratively to help people find and train for good jobs and to ensure that employers can find the skilled workers they need. As described further below, the Administration is:

1. Providing LEADERSHIP in defining best practices with the Job-Driven Checklist.

2. Encouraging INNOVATION to develop more effective models.

3. Spurring COLLABORATION within federal training programs and among states.

2.1. PROVIDING LEADERSHIP IN CREATING A JOB-DRIVEN CHECKLIST

To respond to this call to action, the Departments of Labor, Commerce, and Education worked together with the Departments of Health and Human Services, Housing and Urban Development, VA, Justice, Transportation, Interior, and Agriculture to define what job-driven training is, in accordance with the objectives laid out in the Presidential Memorandum, and to devise a plan to incorporate these job-driven characteristics into training programs across the government.

Working with the Vice President's office, the National Economic Council, the Domestic Policy Council, the Council of Economic Advisers, the Office of Science and Technology Policy, and the Office of Management and Budget, these agencies developed a Job-Driven Checklist that includes seven important features that are an essential part of job-driven training. These elements were chosen based on an understanding of the evidence as represented in _What Works in Job Training: A Synthesis of Evidence._ Many government programs already include some of these features, but there is a great deal of room for improvement. Agencies plan to incorporate these features into their training programs to the maximum extent possible in the coming year.

✓ ENGAGING EMPLOYERS
Work up-front with employers to determine local hiring needs and design training programs that are responsive to those needs – from which employers will hire. Job-driven training begins with working with employers, industry associations, and labor unions early in the process of designing education and training programs. Training programs should coordinate with employers to make sure they are training individuals with skills that have a high likelihood of leading to employment. Programs should also seek employer commitments to contribute to the program through the provision of work-based learning opportunities and/or commitments to hire program graduates.

Engaging Health Care Employers in Milwaukee

The Milwaukee Area Workforce Investment Board partners with Aurora Health Care (Aurora), a local employer, to provide certified nursing assistant training. The WIB works with Aurora to understand the skills that nursing assistants need and trains students in a hospital setting, providing them with hands-on learning opportunities. Because of the relationship with employers and the work-based learning, graduates of the program are more likely to get job offers from area hospitals. More than half of the students in the training are employed by Aurora, and many others are hired by other health care employers or choose to pursue further training and education.

✓ EARN AND LEARN
Offer work-based learning opportunities with employers – including on-the-job training, internships, pre-apprenticeships and Registered Apprenticeships – as training paths to employment. While classroom time can be important, individuals learn best by doing, and individuals can quickly learn skills where hands-on experience in a work environment is integrated with classroom learning. Job-driven training programs should aim to include work-based learning opportunities that best suit their programs. These can include paid internships, pre-apprenticeships, Registered Apprenticeships, and on-the-job training.

Earn and Learn Apprenticeship in Pennsylvania

In apprenticeship programs, individuals are hired and earn wages while they participate in training that leads to higher-wage jobs. The MANUFACTURING 2000 (M2K) entry level machining program, run by New Century Careers, is an apprenticeship program that recruits un/underemployed and low-income individuals and provides hands-on training developed in collaboration with industry in addition to technical math, machine theory, blueprint reading, and metrology. Skills are verified through National Institute of Metals Working Skills standards and credentials. An employer expo upon completion of the program provides on-site interviewing, employment offers, and indefinite job placement assistance. Fees are paid by partner companies that hire M2K graduates help sustain the program.

✓ SMART CHOICES

Make better use of data to drive accountability, inform what programs are offered and what is taught, and offer user-friendly information for job seekers to choose programs and pathways that work for them and are likely to result in jobs. In order to determine what skills should be taught and to guide job seekers as they choose what to study and where to apply for jobs, programs should make better use of data to understand current and projected local, regional, state, and national labor markets. These data may include information on the number and types of jobs available, as well as those jobs' characteristics and skills requirements. These data should be publicly available and easily accessible by job seekers.

Data-Driven Decisions in Stockton, CA

San Joaquin Delta College in Stockton, California eliminated seven of its programs based on a review process that used labor market data. One program eliminated, banking and finance, was a small program that generated only 16 full-time equivalent student enrollments in 2011-2012. Most bank teller jobs require training by the financial institution in question, so the value of the associate's degree was questionable. According to data from California's Employment Development Department, only 53 openings were expected in the banking field in San Joaquin County over the decade between 2008 and 2018. The college determined that many of those jobs would be filled by those with at least a bachelor's degree or higher and eliminated the associate's degree. The college's process fits with the Doing What Matters framework, which California community college leaders are promoting across the state. The framework encourages schools to prioritize programs that lead to jobs and fuel economic growth and retool or eliminate programs that are not relevant in the labor market.

✓ MEASUREMENT MATTERS

Measure and evaluate employment and earnings outcomes. Knowing the outcomes of individual job-driven training programs – how many people become and stay employed and what they earn – is important both to help job seekers decide what training to pursue and to help programs continuously adjust to improve outcomes. Training programs should measure outcomes, evaluate their programs, and convey this information to participants and employers.

Report Cards in New Jersey

New Jersey has a "consumer report card" website called New Jersey Training Opportunities that provides information on occupational training programs in the state. A results section displays information about former program participants. It shows employment rates, retention rates, and average earnings at six months, one year, and two years after graduation. New Jersey's state laws require training programs at for-profit, public two-year, and some public four-year schools that receive state or federal workforce funding to submit records to the state for all of their students. In addition, New Jersey is now implementing a state law that requires all for-profit schools to submit student records and disseminate results through a state website.

✔ STEPPING STONES

Promote a seamless progression from one educational stepping stone to another, and across work-based training and education, so individuals' efforts result in progress. Individuals should have the opportunity to progress in their careers by obtaining new training and credentials. Job-driven training programs should make it easy for individuals to transition from one post-secondary program to another, including Registered Apprenticeships and occupational training programs, and from basic education programs into post-secondary programs.

Stepping Stones in the Virginia Peninsula

The Virginia Peninsula Career Pathways initiative is meeting manufacturers' workforce needs by engaging a consortium of 14 major employers, along with the local Workforce Investment Board, labor unions, community colleges, and six school districts, among other partners. Based on in-depth interviews with employers, the initiative developed 11 career pathway profiles representing more than 11,000 jobs in advanced and precision manufacturing technologies on the Virginia Peninsula, and documenting necessary educational levels, credentials, and work experience requirements. The initiative takes workers where they are and helps them progress from essential skills and basic education to classroom and on-the-job training resulting in credentials and leading to employment and continual on-the-job skills upgrade and advancement, including through Registered Apprenticeships.

✔ OPENING DOORS

Break down barriers to accessing job-driven training and hiring for any American who is willing to work, including access to supportive services and relevant guidance. In order for training programs to work, they need to be accessible for the people who need them most. Job-driven training programs should provide needed supportive services such as transportation, child care, and financial and benefits counseling. Programs also should provide accommodations for persons with disabilities (including supported employment services where needed) in order to allow all individuals to benefit from these opportunities.

Breaking Down Barriers in Albany

LaDasia, a single mother with two sons under the age of two, wanted to find training so that she could stop relying on TANF and become financially independent. She enrolled in a certified nursing assistant program at the Albany Community Action Partnership (ACAP), a partner to an HPOG grantee. ACAP has provided intensive case management throughout her participation in the program. During the training, LaDasia's mother was incarcerated and LaDasia needed help to maintain her public assistance and transportation for getting her children to child care. After completing training, ACAP helped her obtain her driver's license and secure full-time employment. LaDasia reached her six-month job retention milestone, but it was not easy. A few months in, her son was diagnosed with autism and she had to juggle his therapy with her job. LaDasia has persisted and has been invited back by the program to share her experiences with others, encouraging them to press on even when the going gets tough.

✓ REGIONAL PARTNERSHIPS
Coordinate American Job Centers, local employers, education and training providers, economic development agencies, and other public and private entities to make the most of limited resources. In addition to working with employers, job-driven training programs should work with a variety of partners including Workforce Investment Boards and the American Job Centers they oversee, higher education institutions, labor organizations, philanthropic organizations, state and local human service agencies, vocational rehabilitation agencies, Medicaid agencies, centers for independent living, supported employment providers, community- and faith-based organizations, and other non-profit organizations. These partners can provide a network of employment, training, and related services that help individuals overcome barriers to becoming and staying employed and serve many vulnerable populations that should be incorporated into job-driven training programs.

Regional Partnerships in Cincinnati

Partners for a Competitive Workforce is a tri-state partnership in the Cincinnati region managed by United Way. The partnership involves 150+ organizations, including employers, workforce boards, chambers, education and training institutions, and community groups and is one of over 40 National Fund for Workforce Solutions sites supported by a group of leading foundations across the country.

The partnership is developing sectoral partnerships in health care, advanced manufacturing, construction, and IT, seeking to identify industry skill needs and develop aligned curricula and career pathways that meet those needs. The partnership has benefited workers, training over 7,800 individuals, with 80percent obtaining employment and 73percent retained for 12 months. The partnership has also delivered results for employers, serving over 750 businesses, reducing turnover and recruitment costs, and leveraging over $40 million in public and private funds. A 2011 quasi-experimental impact study of the effectiveness of the health care, manufacturing, and construction programs by IMPAQ found that all three were effective in assisting unemployed participants to obtain employment in the 12-month follow-up period, and that the health care program in particular was effective in promoting participant employment in its focus industry.

Federal agencies plan to implement these seven job-driven characteristics into all of their training and employment programs to the maximum extent possible. Their strategies for doing this will vary depending on the structure of the programs.

Competitive grants. The federal government funds many competitive grant programs in which it has discretion over the design requirements and assessment criteria for grant awards. For programs like these, agencies will incorporate the job-driven components into both the design and the assessment processes for awarding competitive grants.

Formula grants. The federal government also funds "formula" grant programs, which distribute funds to state and local entities based on established non-competitive criteria like the population, the unemployment rate, or other economic conditions. State and local entities have more control over how these programs operate. Federal agencies can also influence the extent to which formula programs incorporate the job-driven elements and the quality of their implementation through incentives, guidance on how the Job-Driven Checklist can help improve programs, and dissemination of best practices.

Contracted programs. Finally, some federal programs are run by federal staff or by federal contractors. Depending on the terms of the contract, the federal government should have broad control over how these programs are run and will have an easier time implementing the job-driven elements than in programs that are run at the state or local levels.

The Office of Management and Budget issued a memorandum to executive departments and agencies setting forth the seven job-driven elements, as well as a "checklist" of concrete steps these agencies can take in competitive, formula, and federally run programs. The memorandum directs agencies to incorporate these elements into every employment and training program to the extent practicable and feasible within the law and the program's mission. The memorandum also emphasized the need to measure employment outcomes (e.g., whether program graduates get and keep jobs). Most federal agencies have the authority to add such measures to both their competitive and formula grants. All job-training programs that have the authority to do so will measure and report on employment outcomes, including an additional seven programs that will establish or improve their reporting.

Maximize the Effectiveness of Over 25 Competitive Grant Programs

The federal Government has a great deal of discretion in its competitive grant programs and plans to use this discretion to ensure that training programs funded by competitive grants are job-driven. OMB is calling on federal agencies to implement this checklist into competitive grants (to the extent statutorily permitted) in one of three ways.

1. Required strategies or conditions of grant award. The checklist elements may be required strategies for applicants. For example, applicants could be required to demonstrate their abilities to use local labor market information to assess which jobs are hiring in the local economy. Implementation of some checklist elements may also be pre-conditions for applicants to be considered for a grant awards.

2. Putting in allocation criteria. Agencies may choose to put the checklist elements in the scoring criteria. Applicants would be awarded points for committing to engage in activities aligned with the elements and could be awarded additional points for demonstrating a capacity to implement the checklist more fully. For example, applicants engaging employers fully in curriculum design could be awarded additional points.

3. Bonus points. Agencies could provide bonus points to applicants that address the checklist elements or establish priorities for projects that advance the job-driven elements, giving such applicants an improved chance of receiving grant awards.

Any one or a combination of these approaches could be used within a given grant program. Agencies will be required to implement the checklist into their competitive grant applications starting with applications for funding available after October 1st, 2014. About $1.4 billion in competitive grants will be given out next year. This is in addition to $950 million in grants that have already been launched and were formulated with the Job-Driven Checklist, for a total of $2.4 billion over a two-year period.

This strategy will lead to positive changes among government grantees but more importantly will impact all the organizations applying for federal government funding. At the same time these organizations seek out industry partners to meet these job-driven objectives, the White House is taking on outreach to industry to participate in these grant programs.

Implementing the Job-Driven Checklist in Existing Grants

In addition, the checklist has already been implemented in a number of competitive grants for which applications have been released, totaling over $950 million. Three grants in particular have been used to catalyze partnerships with industry and address major priorities – Trade Adjustment Assistance Community College Training grants ($450 million), Ready to Work Partnership grants ($150 million), and Youth CareerConnect grants ($107 million) – and are covered elsewhere in this report.

The Administration has also implemented the Job-Driven Checklist in a number of grants aside from these major three grants. Some of these grants have already produced successful grantees.

Reintegration of Ex-Offenders. The Training to Work Adult Reintegration of Ex-Offenders (RExO) grants require grantees to establish Career Pathways Collaborative (CPC) steering committees, each of which includes a grantee (a non-profit), the workforce system including employer-led Workforce Investment Boards, the work release program (WRP), and multiple employers or industry groups. A career pathway must train for in-demand occupations, with evidence on the local labor market provided, and employers must validate these data. The employers must be engaged in defining the career pathways, confirming the skills and credentials required for the occupations chosen, and playing a role in curriculum design and instruction. Employer-partners are required to put something on the table, which could include work-based learning opportunities such as paid work or on-the-job training.

The Dannon Project in Birmingham, AL

The Dannon Project is a non-profit organization in Birmingham, AL committed to improving the health, educational, and financial well-being of all at-risk populations, specifically non-violent ex-offenders. The Dannon Project was recently awarded a Training to Work RExO grant to develop and implement a career pathway program in in-demand sectors and occupations for men and women who are enrolled in work release programs, with priority given to veterans returning to the Birmingham area. The certification programs offered are Customer Service, Retail, Forklift, Front Desk, Guest Room Attendant, Maintenance, Nursing, Green Building Basics, Patient Care Tech, Phlebotomy, and a Commercial Construction/Electrical apprenticeship. Participants will receive certifications to ease their entry into in-demand occupations that lead to rewarding careers. As a part of the grant, the Dannon Project will lead a Career Pathways Collaborative that brings together representatives from the workforce system, employers, local community colleges and four-year universities and employers. Each of these organizations has a role to play in providing an integrated set of critical participant-level services such as case management and skills training that allow participants to get on career pathways and advance along those pathways as they acquire additional skills.

The Face Forward Youth RExO grants are designed to equip court-involved youth with skills that increase their ability to find work and earn higher wages by meeting the skill requirements of actual jobs that employers either are filling now or anticipate filling in the future. These grants will build on existing promising practices, such as earning industry-recognized credentials in in-demand occupations and sectors, providing on-the-job training and work-based learning opportunities, and strengthening industry and employer connections to ensure that the training program directly aligns with the skills and credentials needed to secure employment. Successful grantees will use real-time labor market information to make the best choices about training in in-demand sectors and occupations. Grantees will share this labor market information with youth participants so they understand what it takes to get hired and earn enough to thrive in their communities as productive citizens throughout their lifetimes.

Homeless Veterans' Reintegration Program. The Homeless Veterans' Reintegration Program (HVRP) grants support programs that provide job training, counseling, and placement services to expedite the reintegration of homeless veterans into the labor force. This year's HVRP grant solicitation targets job-driven training programs for homeless veterans, requiring that grant applicants promote active engagement with industry, employers and employer associations to identify the skills needed for in-demand jobs and careers. Programs funded by the grant must include training that is targeted to specific industries, occupations, and skills in demand, training strategies that are geared towards providing skills development for jobs currently available, and work-based learning opportunities such as Registered Apprenticeships, paid internships, on-the-job training, cooperative learning, work experience, and customized training.

Job-Driven National Emergency Grants. This year, DOL provided almost $155 million in National Emergency Grant (NEG) funds to 34 entities, including 32 states, one territory and one federally-recognized tribe. In order to qualify for funding, the grantees had to partner with employers and 30 percent of the funds had to be used for work-based training strategies. Applicants were asked to develop job-driven strategies that meet the needs of dislocated workers, including recently unemployed individuals impacted by layoffs, long-term unemployed workers, foreign-trained immigrants, and recipients of unemployment insurance that are likely to exhaust their benefits.

The grant strategy was successful, and recipients of these NEGs are implementing a number of job-driven strategies for dislocated workers.

- Thanks to the requirement that grantees use work-based training strategies, 21 grantees are using the funds to expand Registered Apprenticeships, including three that are creating new Registered Apprenticeship programs, and a number of states are implementing sector strategies in industries like transportation and logistics.

- The grants are also helping to expand successful models. For example, Nevada will help expand the Platform to Employment model to help the long-term unemployed get back to work. Vermont will expand the Vermont HITEC model into the state's American Job Centers to serve long-term unemployed workers. HITEC is an innovative accelerated training and work-based learning model to help unemployed individuals obtain jobs in healthcare information technology.

- A number of grantees are also supporting foreign-trained immigrants, who qualify as dislocated workers, use the skills they obtained in their former countries to fill critical job openings in the United States. For example, Idaho will support the Global Talent Idaho initiative, which provides foreign-trained immigrants with specialized training to hone key job readiness skills such as business communication, interviewing, and networking. Maryland and Washington State will support the expansion of Welcome Back Centers in their states. Welcome Back Centers are a national model with program sites in eight states that help foreign-trained health care professionals obtain state licenses to continue their work in their new homes. The program also provides English as a Second Language and other immigrant integration training services.

Disability Employment Initiative. This fall, grants will be awarded to expand the capacity of American Job Centers to improve employment outcomes of individuals with disabilities (including those with significant disabilities) by increasing the participation of this population in existing career pathways programs that provide a full education and training programs along with supportive services. These programs are being successfully implemented in the public workforce system in partnership with community colleges and other education partners, human services, businesses, and other partners. In addition to the focus on reducing barriers faced by this population, the grant has a job-driven focus by promoting more active engagement with the business sector to identify the skills and support workers with disabilities need and to better communicate these skills to the workforce system and its partners. Additionally, work-based training approaches are encouraged, including on-the-job training, summer youth employment, Registered Apprenticeships, internships, and other paid work experiences

Pathways to Careers for Youth and Young Adults with Disabilities. The Pathways to Careers: Community College for Youth and Young Adults with Disabilities Project is a grant recently released by the Office of Disability Employment Policy at DOL. This fall, grant awards will be made to build on the capacity of the Trade Adjustment Assistance Community College and Career Training grants by awarding funding to two prior grantees to develop, test, and evaluate new integrated education and career training strategies to help ensure that youth and young adults with disabilities acquire the skills, degrees, and credentials needed for high-wage, high-skill employment.

Training Paraprofessionals for the Health Workforce. Through these grants available from HHS in FY 2014, health professions schools, their partner communities, and technical and tribal colleges will work with local government and employers to identify critical needs for paraprofessionals, and then the schools will provide classroom and on-the-job training to help students get the certificates required for those jobs. The students will also get career coaching and placement support to help them find jobs quickly. The program will have a special focus on training people from underrepresented, disadvantaged, and rural backgrounds, and on helping people find work in underserved communities.

Job-Driven Training Grants on the Horizon

Going forward, we have a number of grant competitions that will be launched with job-driven principles. These include the SNAP Employment & Training pilots and performance partnership pilots discussed further below as well as the following grants:

American Apprenticeship Grants. DOL is making $100 million in existing H-1B funds available for American Apprenticeship Grants to reward partnerships that help more workers participate in Registered Apprenticeships. The new grant competition, which will be launched in the fall, is job-driven. It will focus on partnerships between employers, labor organizations, training providers, community colleges, local and state governments, the workforce system (including employer-led Workforce Investment Boards, non-profits and faith-based organizations). These partnerships will launch apprenticeships in high-growth fields, align apprenticeships to pathways for further learning and career advancement, and scale apprenticeship models that have worked. Attention will be focused on encouraging apprenticeship participation by groups that have been underrepresented, including women.

Rural Network Allied Health Training Program. HHS is creating a new program in FY 2015, the Rural Network Allied Health Training Program, to support the development of formal, mature rural health networks. An application for the grant will be available in December 2014. The program will connect rural veterans and displaced workers with training and job-placement opportunities in formal allied health training programs with rural, community-based clinical rotations. The program will also develop a wide and extensive array of collaborative public-private relationships with various community organizations, such as Workforce Investment Boards, academic institutions, and Area Health Education Centers. These collaborative relationships with various community organizations, in particular businesses and health care providers, will be critical in order to ensure community investment in the workforce and to help address mutual workforce challenges.

Encourage State and Local Training and Employment Programs to Become More Job-Driven

A large share of federal job training funds are awarded non-competitively based on factors like the population, the unemployment rate, or other economic conditions. For these programs, federal agencies have less of an ability to direct the adoption of job-driven elements but can impose certain requirements and provide information to state and local grantees on what works well and how they can be more job-driven.

Requiring that States Include the Job-Driven Checklist Elements in their Workforce Innovation and Opportunity Act State Plans

The Workforce Investment Act of 1998, which has recently been reauthorized by the Workforce Innovation and Opportunity Act, created a system of state and local Workforce Investment Boards (WIBs). These WIBs, along with state agencies and governors, are responsible for running the approximately 2,500 American Job Centers across the country that offer employment services and job training. Each of these American Job Centers serves as a one-stop center for job seekers, and together, the American Job Centers served about 18.6 million people in 2012. American Job Centers are required to enable access to a number of resources, including business services; skill assessments; information about local education and training service providers; help in filing claims for unemployment insurance; career counseling, including counseling on non-traditional occupations and up-to-date labor market information on employment trends, local vacancies, and skills necessary for in-demand jobs. These services may be funded through the Adult, Youth, and Dislocated Worker programs; Adult Education; Temporary Assistance for Needy Families; or other programs that are co-located at American Job Centers. The Adult, Youth, and Dislocated Worker programs overseen by DOL serve 8 million individuals, including those that receive virtual services. Nearly 2 million individuals received staff-assisted services at American Job Centers between April 2012 and May 2013 (the most recent data available), and 214,000 of them received training.

The Workforce Innovation and Opportunity Act requires states to develop unified plans across all WIOA-authorized programs. This complements the Administration's job-driven training efforts by requiring these programs to be more coordinated and aligned within each state. DOL will issue guidance to state workforce agencies and Workforce Investment Boards to incorporate the Job-Driven Checklist elements into their operations. Unified state plans will be required to be submitted to the Secretaries of Labor and Education within the next two years. Prior to plan submission, DOL and ED will issue guidance on how the states should incorporate the Job-Driven Checklist into their new plans. Asking states to incorporate the Job-Driven Checklist into their plans should lead them to review their own programs, determine which best meet the job-driven goals, and figure out ways to spread best practices across their states, resulting in better services for individuals and employers.

Using Waivers to Promote the Job-Driven Approach

The Workforce Investment Act authorizes DOL to waive some rules that apply to DOL programs at the request of states. These waivers range from waivers of procurement requirements to waivers that directly relate to training, such those relating to waivers of the maximum employer reimbursement amount for on-the-job training. States use the flexibility afforded by waivers to implement initiatives within State Strategic Plans and to improve the statewide workforce investment system for both job seekers and employers. As a commitment to job-driven training, DOL will now ask that states demonstrate how they are achieving job-driven goals, such as engaging in sector partnerships, prioritizing work-based learning approaches, and making data available on training provider outcomes when states apply for waivers as authorized under the Workforce Innovation and Opportunity Act.

Integrating the Job-Driven Checklist into Economic Development

DOC has made a skilled workforce a central priority. Although DOC does not fund training programs, the department's Economic Development Administration (EDA) funds economic development capacity-building efforts that help communities with strategic planning to identify regional assets and vulnerabilities, including the status of the workforce; technical assistance to improve economic development decision-making, such as workforce needs assessments; and construction assistance to help build foundational physical infrastructure, such as workforce training centers. These activities are crucial in helping communities build the capacity to support a workforce that is attractive to business growth and investment. Without these activities and investments, businesses may not have access to the skilled workforce they need to compete in the global economy.

The U.S. Economic Development Administration (EDA) helps regional planning organizations with their economic development efforts, including the creation of regional economic development plans called Comprehensive Economic Development Strategies (CEDS). EDA will include job-driven training principles in its new CEDS content guidelines, which provide recommendations and tools to help regions develop strong CEDS. These new content guidelines will be released in fall of 2014 and will be available to the over 380 current regional planning organizations as they implement and update their CEDS as well as to any community looking to develop an impactful economic development strategy for its region. The result should be the development or updating of many CEDS with strong, job-driven workforce development language, similar to the CEDS developed by Centralina Economic Development Commission (see box to the left).

EDA also fosters economic development capacity-building efforts in regions through competitive grant investments that spur job creation and attract private investment. EDA has established "job-driven skills development" as an investment priority for its competitive grants. Potential applicants proposing workforce development-related projects that adhere to job-driven skills principles automatically meet an initial evaluation requirement within EDA's grant application review process. EDA's investment priorities are designed to provide an overarching framework for the agency's investment portfolio to ensure its various economic development grant programs have the greatest impact. To be competitive for EDA assistance, grant applications must align with at least one of EDA's investment priorities.

In 2014, the National Institute of Standards and Technology's Manufacturing Extension Partnership (MEP) is beginning a multi-year process of formally re-competing the national system of Centers, with the primary objective of using this process to optimize the impact of the federal investment. The goal is to complete re-competition of the entire 50 state (plus Puerto Rico) national network by FY 2017. To ensure that this process can be implemented without disrupting the MEP system or degrading the program's performance, MEP will initiate a demonstration program in six to 10 states in the summer of 2014. The demonstration program will enable procedures, milestones, and resource requirements to be tested and refined. The demonstration program will be conducted through the release of a new federal Funding Opportunity announcement in August 2014. MEP is committed to including several of the major elements of the job-driven training checklist in the FFO.

Make Sure Programs Serving All Workers Are Engaging Employers

Employers represent over half of the membership of Workforce Investment Boards, and on these boards they provide input on strategic planning as well as specific occupational training. The depth of employer engagement varies across WIBs and across the broader universe of federal training and employment programs, but is critical to success of these programs. A central part of the job-driven agenda is improving business engagement and responsiveness to business needs be across all programs.

Promoting and Measuring Employer Engagement across the Entire WIA System. A first step to improvement of business engagement is measurement. DOL has begun working with Workforce Investment Boards, states, localities, and other stakeholders to identify an approach to measuring business engagement. The Workforce Investment and Opportunity Act has affirmed the importance of this endeavor, requiring the Secretaries to develop a measure of business engagement effectiveness by June 2016. This measure will then be used for all WIOA programs, including vocational rehabilitation and adult education.

Business engagement metrics should incentivize strategic and effective engagement to promote continuous improvement of business services. The federal-state partnership will focus on a measure to reflect the work that is done across the country for this important stakeholder, but will also recognize that a number of states and localities have developed measures that take into account their unique relationships and labor markets that exist at the state and local levels. Some states have already started working on measures of business engagement. For example, Colorado is collaborating with a team of WIBs, businesses, and other stakeholders to implement standardized reporting measures to better understand the state's performance on business services as well as business customer satisfaction. Colorado is counting the services it delivers to businesses, such as help responding to expected layoffs, labor market data, information on eligibility for taxes, business education on compliance with labor laws, job postings/fill rates, job fairs, and training/retraining. For most of the services the state is counting, it has a series of related customer satisfaction measures rated on a scale of 1-5, such as how useful or satisfied the customer was with the services, how likely the customer is to use the services again, and how likely would the customer be to refer someone else.

Enhancing the Role of Employers and Work-Based Learning in Vocational Rehabilitation through Counselor Training and Guidance

The Vocational Rehabilitation (VR) State Grants program under Title I of the Rehabilitation Act supports VR services through grants to state VR agencies. These agencies provide a wide range of VR services to assist adults and youth with disabilities, including those with significant disabilities, to prepare for, obtain, or retain gainful employment commensurate with their capabilities, including full-time or part-time competitive employment in the integrated labor market; supported employment; or other employment including self-employment or business ownership. The Vocational Rehabilitation program serves over one million individuals per year with disabilities.

ED is taking a number of steps to increase the role of employers and the connection to work-based learning.

Reforming the System of Training Vocational Rehabilitation Counselors. ED provides grants to colleges that train VR counselors and also provides $33.6 million in funding to VR agencies to administer training for counselors. ED is making sure that this funding is being spent to make the VR program more job-driven. ED will ask universities applying for $34 million to train VR counselors to address how their curricula help VR counselors build and maintain relationships with employers by teaching successful approaches to working with employers to provide job opportunities for persons with disabilities. This will include teaching counselors how to understand data about job trends and industry and occupational classification systems, a knowledge base that is necessary for them to engage effectively with employers, as well as knowledge about ways to customize employment for individuals with disabilities.

Technical Assistance Center Focused on Job-Driven Activities. The Rehabilitation Services Administration anticipates funding a technical assistance center that will support state VR agencies to (a) improve the ability of state VR agencies to work with employers and providers of training to ensure equal access to, and greater opportunities for, individuals with disabilities to engage in competitive employment or training; (b) increase the number and quality of employment outcomes in competitive, integrated settings for VR-eligible individuals with disabilities; and (c) increase the number of VR-eligible individuals with disabilities in employer-driven job training programs.

Guidance on Integrated Employment. In FY 2015, ED/RSA will issue guidance on integrated employment, focusing on VR program integrated employment requirements to better enable grantees to identify job opportunities in the community that afford individuals with disabilities full interaction with non-disabled employees. The guidance also strongly encourages the use of community-based training and work experiences to prepare individuals for integrated employment, rather than sheltered settings in which individuals with disabilities are segregated and have little exposure to work settings in the community. For example, the Delaware Division of Vocational Rehabilitation (DVR) administers the Team Approach to Reaching Goals through Education and Training (TARGET) program in partnership with the Delaware Department of Labor. This program provides at-risk students with disabilities, including recipients of social security benefits (SSI/SSDI) and those exiting correctional institutions, employment services, such as job seeking skills, placement services and internship opportunities in collaboration with local employers. This guidance will explain the benefits of job skills training and work experience in community-based settings rather than sheltered settings.

Walgreens Employing People with Disabilities

Walgreens has demonstrated a commitment to offering employment opportunities for people with disabilities while making their operations more efficient. Walgreens Distribution Centers are the foundation of the retail chain. Walgreens senior vice president of supply chain and logistics Randy Lewis wanted to make these centers operate more smoothly while employing people with disabilities.

Walgreens worked with specialists in the vocational rehabilitation field and opened a state-of-the-art distribution center in Anderson, SC in 2007. The center features a work environment designed to be inclusive for people with cognitive or physical disabilities, with the following accommodations: flexible workstations, elevators for those who can't walk up the steps, touch-screen computers with large icons and easy-to-read type for the visually impaired, and new systems designed to help all team members work efficiently.

As of October 2011 (the latest date for which they published data), 9.5 percent of distribution center jobs were held by people who have disabilities. The goal is to fill 20 percent of distribution center jobs with people who have disabilities.

"Our employees with disabilities earn the same pay, work under the same standards and work side-by-side with all other employees," said Lewis. "This is a business, not a charity. And it has turned out better than we could've ever imagined."

Employer Engagement Roundtable. In 2015, ED, together with other federal agencies, will convene an Employer Engagement Roundtable that brings business leaders and VR professionals and others together to develop strategies to ensure that individuals with disabilities, including those with the most significant disabilities, have the necessary skills to obtain meaningful jobs in today's economy.

Improving Adult Education Providers' Efforts to Teach Employability Skills

ED's Adult Education program provides basic education and English literacy skills to 1.7 million out-of-school youth and adults each year. Last year, nearly half of the participants (48 percent) enrolled in adult basic education, which provides basic skills instruction below the high school level. Another 40 percent enrolled in English language acquisition instruction, and 12 percent enrolled in adult secondary education, which provides instruction at the high school level.

Employers are seeking workers who have employability skills like critical thinking and communication. Later this year, ED will issue state plan guidance that will require states to address how they will incorporate employability skills development in the state plans they will submit in April 2015. This will build on the work ED has been doing to provide technical assistance to states on how to incorporate employability skills development into their programs.

Showcasing Employer Engagement Across Department of Education Programs. By the end of this year, ED will develop a tool kit and vignettes that show effective employer engagement drawing on the best practices in adult education, career and technical education, and vocational rehabilitation. This will build on work that ED has done as a part of its career pathway initiative. ED developed an issue brief and an online course that offered practical strategies on engaging employers and forging business-education partnerships.

Deepening Relationships with Businesses to Hire Veterans and Connecting Veterans to Occupational Training

Providing education and training opportunities to our veterans is a priority across the federal government. VA, DOL, and ED all play important roles in making sure that veterans have full access to education and training opportunities as well as the supportive services that will help them to be successful in civilian life.

All veterans receive priority of service for DOL-funded employment and training programs. Post 9-11 veterans are also eligible for Gold Card services – six months of services that include skills assessments, job search assistance, and career guidance. In addition, the Veterans Employment Training Service within DOL conducts the Jobs for Veterans State Grants (JVSG) program, which funds employment counselors through the Disabled Veterans' Outreach Program (DVOP) that work at American Job Centers and are solely responsible for serving veterans with significant barriers to employment. The VETS office also funds Local Veterans Employment Representatives (LVERs) who are responsible for engaging businesses to identify job opportunities for veterans. Together these JVSG funds are serving approximately 1.3 million veterans per year. Additionally, many veterans choosing to pursue education or training may have access to the GI Bill, which covers certain education and training programs approved for VA education purposes. Veterans with service-connected disabilities are also eligible to receive services through the Vocational Rehabilitation & Employment (VR&E) program. Following a comprehensive evaluation, eligible and entitled veterans receive individualized services that may include career exploration and counseling, educational, vocational, or on-the- job training, case management, adjustment counseling, and job readiness and job placement. In FY 2013, about 136,000 veterans participated in the VR&E program.

Both the VR&E and the VETS programs are taking steps to make the services that Veterans receive more job-driven.

Deepening Relationships with Businesses to Hire Veterans. VETS is establishing a Job Development Unit that will collect employment commitments from national and regional employers seeking to hire veterans, including those federal contractors responsible for making efforts to meet hiring targets established under a recent set of regulations. The new Job Development Unit will connect these employers with Business Engagement Teams at American Job Centers and Local Veterans Employment Representatives specifically responsible for local business outreach on behalf of hiring veterans.

Connecting the VA Vocational Rehabilitation and Employment to American Job Centers. The Vocational Rehabilitation and Employment (VR&E) program within VA will work with VETS in DOL to update the National Memorandum of Agreement to frame how Vocational Rehabilitation Counselors can leverage labor market and career information and employer relationships from state workforce investment boards to connect veterans with disabilities to in-demand training and employment opportunities. Each VA Regional Office will then update its local MOU with the appropriate Directors for Veterans' Employment and Training in each state. The DOL/VA Joint Working Group will also update the joint Technical Assistance Guide, which describes the standard operating procedures for all partners, including VETS, VR&E, and each State Agency who work with veterans in the VR&E program, to reflect the job-driven training initiatives described above.

Engaging Employers in Training for Refugee Resettlement and Job Placement

The Office of Refugee Resettlement (ORR) plans to engage employers more by increasing outreach through Regional Representatives and increasing support for Refugee State Coordinators and services providers. Through technical assistance ORR is able to match companies with prospective employees and provide support services that improve job retention rates. This is accomplished through partnerships with local resettlement agencies and ethnic-community organizations along with an in-depth knowledge of local labor market conditions and corporate staffing needs.

Improve Information on Employment Results

Central to the concept of job-driven training is whether training programs actually help participants find and keep good jobs. Program operators need this information in order to improve their programs and individuals need it to be able to make informed choices among programs.

Requiring Employment Measures for All Training Programs

In order to determine whether training programs actually help participants find and keep good jobs, programs need to track their participants' outcomes using at least three core measures: how many participants find jobs, how many of them stay employed, and how much they earn in those jobs. Programs should make information on each of these outcomes readily available to participants and policy-makers and use this information to inform their program operations and continuously improve program performance.

While many federal employment and training programs already track such employment outcomes, several others either do not track, or only partially track, employment outcomes of participants in their programs. WIOA has required that all programs authorized under that bill include employment outcomes, including two programs at ED which do not currently track the full range of employment outcomes measures: Vocational Rehabilitation and Adult Education, which total $3.9 billion in annual funding. In addition, the following programs, totaling nearly $3 billion in annual funding, will either begin tracking or substantially improve their measurement of the core employment outcomes:

VA	Dept. of Labor	Dept. of Defense	Dept. of Justice	Dept. of Agriculture
Veterans Vocational Rehabilitation & Employment	Homeless Veterans' Reintegration Program	Youth ChalleNGe	Reentry & Training	SNAP Employment & Training

Requiring Education and Training Providers to Report on Participant Outcomes

Both the Workforce Innovation and Opportunity Act and the Higher Education Act (and the regulations that implement these acts) provide opportunities to ensure that occupational training programs meet baseline performance standards that help provide assurance to participants and taxpayers that these programs meet a basic level of quality. In order for individuals to obtain information on program effectiveness, training providers must be required to report their results. In our economy, training providers include a wide range of institutions, and these institutions are subject to different rules about reporting key outcomes like employment rates and earnings. Requirements on reporting of outcomes for community colleges are set by the college or the state. Some for-profit schools are subject to state and federal reporting but others are not. Individuals who do go through training offered at American Job Centers receive vouchers that are often used at community colleges, but community colleges are not the only providers. For example, small community-based organizations may work with employers to offer training. The Workforce Innovation and Opportunity Act governs what outcomes these training providers have to report. In addition, many individuals get vocational training without ever going through our federal training programs by paying tuition at community colleges or for-profit schools. Additionally, under the Higher Education Act, there are particular programs that by design should lead to gainful employment in recognized occupations as a condition of eligibility to participate in the federal Student Financial Aid programs.

Getting to a point where individuals have information to make an educated choice between all programs – whether offered through an American Job Center, the community college a friend went to, or the for-profit for which they saw an advertisement – requires bringing together multiple systems that are currently disconnected. Federal agencies with education and training programs recognize the importance of achieving these goals and are taking steps to move toward a more integrated system in which all training providers are required to report outcomes.

Eligible Training Providers under the Workforce Investment Act. DOL will no longer issue state plan waivers that allow a state to extend the period of initial eligibility for training providers under the Workforce Investment Act and its successor statute, the Workforce Innovation and Opportunity Act. Without this waiver, training providers would be required to report employment and earnings outcome data for all the students they serve. Making such information available will allow prospective trainees to make better choices about which programs to attend and help states determine which programs are of sufficiently high quality to receive training funds. Similarly, providing more information about programs' track records of success will allow individuals who receive federally-funded job training vouchers to make smarter, well informed choices about which programs to attend.

In addition, WIOA requires that DOL issue a standardized format – or scorecard – that all Eligible Training Providers will use to display and disseminate their performance outcomes. DOL will work with ED and other stakeholders to make sure that this format is usable and useful to workers, job seekers, employers, elected officials, policymakers, and other key stakeholders. DOL will publish this template within one year.

Post-Secondary Occupational Programs under the Higher Education Act. Efforts to strengthen information available to participants and policy-makers under the Workforce Investment Act build on the work ED has done to strengthen post-secondary occupational programs at institutions of higher education through its proposed gainful employment regulations.
The proposed regulations are intended to address growing concerns about educational programs that, as a condition of eligibility for Higher Education Act Title IV program funds, are required by statute to provide training that prepares students for gainful employment in recognized occupations (GE programs), but instead are leaving students with unaffordable levels of loan debt in relation to their earnings, or leading to default. The regulations address concerns that too many programs fail to train students in the skills they need to obtain and maintain jobs in their chosen occupations; provide training for occupations for which low wages do not justify program costs; and enroll large numbers of students where very few actually complete the program, often leading to default on their student loans. Additionally, providing clear information about gainful employment program ensures that prospective students and their families are less susceptible to being pressured and misled into critical decisions regarding their educational investments that are against their interests, a concern over growing evidence from federal and state investigations.

Specifically, the regulations define what it means to prepare students for gainful employment in recognized occupations by establishing outcome measures by which ED can evaluate whether a gainful employment program remains eligible for Title IV program funds and requiring programs to report and disclose information about the outcomes of students enrolled in these occupational programs. Better outcome information would benefit students, prospective students, and their families as they make critical decisions about their educational investments. It also helps the public, taxpayers, and the government by providing information that would enable better protection of federal investment in these programs. Finally, it helps institutions that run the programs by providing them with meaningful information that they could use to help improve student outcomes in their programs.

Providing States Assistance in Accessing Wage Data. States trying to facilitate the reporting of employment outcomes often cite the difficulty of accessing the necessary wage data to do so accurately. Yet many states, such as Washington, Florida, and California, have found ways to do this. DOL, HHS, and ED will advise states on methods for linking program participant data with state wage records. South Carolina has recently used this capability so that community colleges can access these data and report on performance.

Expanding Information on Employment Outcomes for Individuals

Providing Individuals Information on How Training Programs Stack Up. DOL is working with five community colleges that have received Trade Adjustment Assistance Community College and Career Training grants to develop new ways to provide information to the public concerning eligible training programs. With these five grantees, DOL will pilot the development of community college training program scorecards. These scorecards will have employment and earnings outcomes for training programs. In addition, DOL is working with Workforce Data Quality Initiative grantees to develop scorecards for their state workforce systems. By 2017, these states will make these scorecards available to the public.

More Comprehensive Reporting on Employment and Earnings Outcomes. In the summer of 2014, DOL began making updates to aggregate performance data on the Trade Adjustment Assistance training program publicly available to employers and workers on a quarterly basis which will be posted on the TAA website to provide reader-friendly data on services, participant outcomes, and performance elements.

Florida's Consumer Report Card System

Florida began developing its longitudinal administrative data infrastructure in the 1970s and has continued to expand the system. The Florida Consumer Report Card System (CRCS) is developed statewide from workforce and education individual-level data. It covers the K-20 education system and workforce data, including UI wage records. The assessment and analysis of participation and outcomes of all education and training programs are conducted exclusively through use of individual-level data from the Florida education and workforce systems. Much of the data analysis connected to the CRCS is conducted by the state. For example, to be put on a local Eligible Training Provider List (ETPL), a training provider must provide a program that trains for an occupation that is on the Targeted Occupations List – termed "demand occupations" – and must be licensed in Florida to be on the ETPL. The Florida College System has developed a website for parents, students, and interested partiesto be able to see recent first-year outcomes by institution and program.

Providing Skills Data to Training Providers. DOC's National Institute of Standards and Technology's Hollings Manufacturing Extension Partnership (MEP) is implementing a data-gathering tool that will help small manufacturers capture their current skill needs as well as their future skill demands. This cloud-based software diagnostic, called SMARTalent, is currently in the pilot phase, but will be gathering real-time data by winter of 2014. The data can inform community colleges, apprenticeship programs, and Workforce Investment Boards about the current and changing skill needs of advanced manufacturing.

Supporting More Job-Driven Approaches through Targeted Technical Assistance and Dissemination of Best Practices

As discussed above, federal agencies work closely with state and local grantees to better understand what works well and how they can move to a more job-driven focus. In almost all cases, local programs want to do as much as they can to help people attain good jobs, but they may need guidance to better work with employers to improve job placement rates or introduce better data about the local labor market to help improve the advice they give to job seekers about which fields of training to pursue.

Coordinated Outreach to Governors and Local Agencies on Job-Driven Training Checklist. As a first step, many agencies are notifying their state and local grantees about the checklist and asking them to incorporate the Job-Driven Checklist into their operations.

Building on the letters that agencies are sending out to program operators and the specific steps that are being taken to deepen employer engagement, work-based learning, and information for individuals, agencies will also take a number of actions to help grantees understand how to incorporate other job-driven practices into their operations and will disseminate best practices that wrap many of the job-driven elements together.

DOL, ED, DOC, and HHS are issuing a joint letter to governors about the Job-Driven Checklist. DOL and ED will follow up this letter with outreach to program operators about the checklist. In September, HHS will be issuing a letter to TANF agencies describing strategies for engaging employers and using better data on job availability. Each month, about one million adults and 1.7 million families receive assistance from TANF and related state programs, many of whom are involved in work or work-related activities including vocational training.

USDA will also send a letter to agencies that administer SNAP. SNAP offers nutrition assistance to millions of eligible, low-income individuals and families and provides economic benefits to communities. USDA will send letters by September 30th to all agencies that administer the SNAP program encouraging them to strengthen job-driven elements into their SNAP Employment and Training (E&T) programs for FY 2015. The letter will emphasize the importance of job-driven E&T programs in connecting SNAP participants with available employment opportunities, helping them attain self-sufficiency, and reducing their need for SNAP benefits. The letter will include examples of best practices and lessons learned.

Helping States Create Career Pathways for Workers of all Skill Levels. DOL will launch the National Career Pathways Peer Network, an initiative to provide states and formula and competitive grantees working with job seekers of varying skill levels an enhanced set of resources and technical assistance to scale the number and quality of state-level career pathways systems in place nationwide. To address the particular needs of lower-skilled job seekers, ED will launch the Career Pathways Exchange, an online information dissemination service that will give all states and interested stakeholders access to resources and guidance to assist them in developing, expanding, and strengthening their career pathways systems.

Helping TANF Agencies Implement Job-Driven Practices. In addition to sending a letter to TANF agencies describing strategies for engaging employers and using better data on job availability, over the next year, HHS will host an 18-month policy academy, "Systems to Family Stability," to work with state and local TANF program directors and their partners to help them strengthen their TANF programs so that they are more effective in improving the economic and social well-being of needy children and their families. In particular, it will focus on integrating client assessment and case management, redesigning client flows or integrating education, training, and employment with a goal of providing entry into the highest-paying and often non-traditional occupations for women and their families. HHS will also disseminate lessons learned from the Health Profession Opportunity Grants (HPOG) program and Responsible Fatherhood program with the broader TANF community through webinars, regional meetings and a National TANF Summit.

Guidance to Help Youth with Disabilities Transfer into the Labor Market. In 2015, ED will issue a Transition Guidance Package. The guidance will encourage collaboration and cooperation among agencies connecting with youth during transition periods including schools, state educational agencies, VR agencies, and adult services. It will also explain how this collaboration can be used to improve the extent to which students with disabilities, including those with the most significant disabilities, receive education and skills demanded by employers and necessary to achieve jobs and careers in today's economy.

Disseminating Job-Driven Best Practices to Tribal leaders and Grantees Serving Native Americans. DOI will use annual reports submitted from tribes participating in employment and training programs to select examples of successful programs and then will disseminate those program models to all tribes so that they have the opportunity to implement those that may help them meet their goals. HHS, which operates the Tribal TANF and Native Employment Works program, will also be hosting a series of technical assistance events focused on helping its grantees implement job-driven practices like job creation through career pathways. HHS has also been assisting tribes operating TANF to implement job-driven strategies and will hold roundtable discussions in August on economic development and subsidized employment.

Connecting Individuals with Disabilities to Employers and Job Driven Community-based Training Opportunities. In 2015, ED will update its guidance to vocational rehabilitation agencies serving individuals with disabilities. Guidance will highlight promising examples of strong employer engagement and community-based training that provide individuals with disabilities, including those with the most significant disabilities, with the skills demanded by employers and needed to obtain jobs available in today's economy.

Guidance on Eligibility of Immigrants for Services. Later this fall the DOL Civil Rights Division will release citizenship guidance to the workforce system outlining the various immigrant groups eligible to receive workforce services, as well as rules against discrimination of these groups. DOL is also planning to release updated data on hired farm workers – many of whom are immigrants from Mexico and Central America – to develop a better understanding of the labor pool available to U.S. agricultural employers.

2.2 FOSTER INNOVATION TO IMPROVE JOB TRAINING

As we spread effective practices, we also need to use our federal programs to start experimenting with new approaches to job training. As a separate report on the evidence for job-driven training documents, there is a need to develop our knowledge base about what works. Major priorities include a focus on two populations where research has failed to produce evidence on effective job strategies – disconnected youth and adult learners with many different barriers to employment. Additionally, although we know that higher education matters – educational attainment is strongly associated with higher earnings – we don't know the best way to help individuals attain skills quickly.

Reforming Job Corps and Testing Models for Disconnected Youth

Job Corps to Test Models for Disconnected Youth. Job Corps is the federal government's largest investment in residential job training for disadvantaged youth. The program aims to help high school drop-outs and unemployed youth ages 16 to 24 train for careers and obtain their high school equivalency or high school diplomas. Research on the program shows that while it increases the education and earnings of program participants, the program is more beneficial for youth over age 20 than for its younger participants. To strengthen the program for youth under age 20, DOL, within the next year, will use Job Corps' demonstration authority to begin the process of testing and evaluating innovative and promising models that could improve the outcomes of these youth. These models may include blended academic and occupational training combined with work experience in high-demand fields, a residential model for at-risk youth with a rigorous academic, college preparatory and career focus, dual enrollment, a military style education and character development model similar to National Guard ChalleNGe, or other innovative models that integrate cognitive and non-cognitive skills training.

Performance Partnership Pilots for Disconnected Youth. In August, ED will be releasing an application for performance partnership pilots. The purpose of these pilots is to improve outcomes for disconnected youth ages 14 to 24 by allowing for the blending of funds across DOL, ED, the Corporation for National and Community Service, and HHS. Disconnected youth are low-income and either homeless, in foster care, involved in the juvenile justice system, unemployed, or not enrolled in or at risk of dropping out of an educational institution. These agencies have also combined grant sources to offer a least $7 million in new funding. In line with the job-driven agenda, these pilots will emphasize the key role of partnerships across youth-serving programs, as well as with private-sector partners. Among the models that states and local governments could test are programs developed in partnerships with employers that build skills and offer work experience for disconnected youth. In addition, the pilots are consistent with WIOA's focus on enhancing outreach and services for disconnected youth to improve their employment outcomes.

National Guard Youth ChalleNGe and Job ChalleNGe Demonstration. DOL is partnering with the National Guard to run a demonstration for improving the long-term labor market prospects of youth with prior involvement in the juvenile justice system by building on the Youth ChalleNGe Program model. The Job ChalleNGe demonstrations will invest $9 million into existing National Guard Youth ChalleNGe programs to build out a more robust employment and training component to the model. Youth ChalleNGe program will have an opportunity to apply for the demonstrations later this summer.

Innovation in Higher Education Financing and Delivery

The President has called on all Americans to get some form of post-secondary training or education. Ensuring all Americans can access quality, affordable post-secondary education opportunities with the skills they need to improve employment prospects requires taking action to promote innovation and competition in the higher education marketplace. To meet this objective, the Administration is taking a number of steps to support higher education institutions that are leading the way on innovations that can lead to breakthroughs on college costs and quality:

Creating Greater Regulatory Flexibility by Pilot Testing New Approaches to Student Financial Aid that Support Innovative Models of Higher Education Delivery Designed to Better Equip Students with Skills Employers are Demanding. This year, ED plans to issue regulatory waivers for "experimental sites" that align with both the Administration's skills training and college affordability agendas. One such experiment would entail providing greater flexibility to colleges to access student aid for programs of study that facilitate students to pursue a more self-paced college experience by demonstrating that they have mastered particular skills and competencies (such as by demonstrating learning directly through projects, papers, examinations, presentations, performances, and/or portfolios) rather than based on how many hours they spend sitting in a classroom. This means that students, particularly adult learners and those employed while in school, will have a greater ability to complete their degrees and obtain good jobs relevant to labor market needs more quickly, and thus more affordably.

Additionally, ED will be providing greater flexibility through experimental sites to encourage colleges to incorporate credit for prior learning achieved through prior learning assessments. For students who have already spent time in the workforce gaining skills, their prior work could be built into their programs of study to accelerate their progress towards credentials or degrees, rather than having to waste time and money on to retake courses in areas where they have already mastered the knowledge. ED also plans to expand participation in two current experimental site pilots in the federal Pell grant program that allow the use of the grant for students in short-term training programs that are meeting critical local or regional workforce needs

Western Governors University

Western Governors University (WGU) is a private, non-profit, online American university based in Salt Lake City, Utah. Established in 1997 by 19 U.S. governors, WGU is the only university in the country offering competency-based degree programs at scale. In 2013, tuition for WGU is $2,890 per six-month term for most undergraduate programs and has not increased since the fall of 2008. The university's sole focus is to provide its students, who are busy adults, with affordable and flexible degree programs.

Because competency-based learning allows students to advance as soon as they demonstrate mastery of course materials, the average time to complete a bachelor's degree at WGU is 34 months, in comparison to 54 months for the average community college student. WGU offers more than 50 bachelor's, master's, and post-baccalaureate degree programs in the key workforce areas of business, information technology, K–12 teacher education, and health professions.

WGU students experienced an average increase in income of $9,000 in the first one to three years after graduation, and an average increase of $18,600 within six years of graduation, significantly higher than the national average. **With an average cost of $18,000 for a bachelor's degree, the return on investment of a WGU degree is 2-3 years.**

Open Educational Resources (OER) Repository Microsite. The Employment and Training Administration is creating a repository microsite that will house hundreds of digital products created using grant funds by the Trade Adjustment Assistance Community College and Career Training grants. These products include learning components for programs of study and courses, such as lesson plans, professional development materials, courses and course modules, institutional research, and evaluation tools. These products incorporated online and/or technology-enabled learning strategies, such as interactive simulations, personalized and virtual instruction, educational gaming, digital tutors, asynchronous and real-time collaboration strategies, and next generation assessments. The Department will use this repository to ensure that all deliverables are publically available as Open Educational Resources (OER) and to provide open discovery services that will enable quick, easy, and reliable access to content by community college students, adult learners, unemployed workers, and other learners, faculty members and instructional designers at other educational institutions, and the workforce system. These Open Educational Resources will then be leveraged by the online skills academy DOL is launching (discussed in chapter 3).

Providing Funding for States to Make SNAP Employment & Training More Job-Driven

Supplemental Nutrition Assistance Program (SNAP) Employment and Training (E&T) Pilots. All recipients of USDA's SNAP benefits, unless exempt, must comply with work requirements such as registering for work, taking a job if offered, not quitting a job, and participating in an E&T program if mandated by the state. In FY 2013, 13.3 million SNAP recipients were registered for work and 633,760 SNAP recipients participated in SNAP E&T activities.[26] SNAP work registrants are a diverse population – some have recent attachment to work, others have been out of work for many years, and still others work at low-paying jobs. In August, USDA will announce a funding opportunity for E&T pilot projects to develop and test strategies designed to increase the number of SNAP work registrants who obtain employment, increase earned income, and reduce reliance on public assistance. This funding opportunity includes $200 million for up to 10 three-year pilots and an independent evaluation. USDA will incorporate Job-Driven Checklist elements in evaluating applications. The pilots require collaboration with workforce boards and emphasize strong supportive services for all participants.

Improving State Job Portals

DOL has announced 12 states that will be receiving technical assistance on improving their use of data to match program participants with available jobs. This technical assistance will help states deliver integrated reemployment services to all jobseekers. It will also help states develop new tools to improve state job portals, including ways to communicate recommended jobs to jobseekers based on their skills, and using social media to make people aware of job opportunities. These improvements will allow the states to connect unemployment insurance recipients more seamlessly to state job portals and to the reemployment services available through American Job Centers. These tools were developed in an early pilot with five states. DOL plans to make these tools available to all states during the summer of 2014. In addition, DOL provided additional funding of $175,000 to each of the 34 grantees that were recently awarded Job-Driven NEGs to undertake activities to better serve dislocated workers, with a focus on increasing consumer access to information and upgrading electronic tools.

---

[26] "Food and Nutrition Service 2015 Explanatory Notes," *U.S. Department of Agriculture.*

2.3 ENCOURAGING COLLABORATION

As we identify effective strategies, it is important to spread those strategies through collaboration. We are working to encourage collaboration and alignment of education, workforce, and economic development at the state and local levels and to model that collaboration at the federal level as well. States have a great deal of influence in whether the programs in the state are job-driven. Governors and state workforce boards can set industry priority areas based on labor market demand. States devote funding to attract businesses to their state, making different choices about how training programs can best support those economic development goals and what level of investment in their workers is expected of businesses. States and local governments can also appropriate additional funding to job training. Some states have created their own grant programs aimed at state priorities.

Workforce Innovation Funds for State-Level Reforms

Targeting $30 million in Workforce Innovation Funding for State Reforms. DOL will announce $30 million in competitive grants for states to align policy, governance, program, and performance measurement across training programs. DOL will send a letter to states about this funding opportunity in the fall of 2014 with an application available in the winter of 2015. Grants will be awarded to five to 10 states. More state winners could follow, if Congress continues to appropriate WIF funding in future budgets.

These grants recognize the discretion states have in organizing their job training systems. They can determine what state departments have authority over programs and can also determine which programs fall under the workforce investment boards. For example, some state TANF agencies have chosen to partner with WIBs and transfer funding to those WIB agencies for direct service delivery.

Minnesota FastTRAC

Minnesota FastTRAC (Training, Resources, and Credentialing) seeks to make Minnesota more competitive by meeting common skills needs of businesses and individuals. FastTRAC's Adult Career Pathways program helps educationally underprepared adults succeed in well-paying careers by integrating basic skills education and career-specific training in high-demand fields. Each local Adult Career Pathways program consists of a series of connected educational and training programs that allow students to advance over time to successively higher levels of education and employment in a given sector. FastTRAC programs cover key Minnesota industries, including health care, manufacturing, education, business, energy, and others. As of December 2012, FastTRAC programs have served over 1,900 adults at 29 sites. Eighty-eight percent of these adults earned industry-recognized credentials or earned credits toward those credentials, and 69 percent had success either gaining employment or continuing into further career pathway education.

Local programs have braided FastTRAC grants with other state and federal funds. Locals have braided funds from TANF, WIA Incentive grants, Adult Basic Education Leadership funds, Perkins funds, foundation funding, Pell grants, and other sources. Currently, an allocation from the state workforce development fund and TANF Innovation funds are braided in the 2014.

Helping States and Localities Understand How Funding across Programs Can be Braided

Combining Funds to Help Lower-Skilled Workers. **States** and cities express challenges in using adult education funding and occupational training funds in programs that blend both basic skills and occupational training. When done successfully, blending results in great programs like Minnesota's FastTRAC initiative, which has served over 3,000 individuals and resulted in an 88 percent completion rate of college credit and/or credential and a 69 percent rate of continuing education and/or obtaining employment. (See sidebar.)

In 2015, ED, in coordination with DOL, will issue guidance and organize a national webinar to illustrate how adult education, career and technical education, and vocational rehabilitation providers can partner with workforce development organizations and business, industry, and labor to support and expand integrated education and training programs. This guidance will address how adult education and occupational training funds can be braided, using each program consistent with its purposes as part of a comprehensive whole, building on the exemplary work that states and local communities that have done in this area.

> **Philadelphia Youth Councils**
>
> Youth Councils are a subgroup of local workforce boards and are responsible for developing the youth-related portion of the local plan, recommending eligible youth service providers, and coordinating local youth programs. The Youth Councils create an opportunity for key stakeholders in the community to create a shared vision for serving disconnected youth that is informed by cross-systems data. Philadelphia's Youth Council is the center of a major collective impact effort. They began the Philadelphia Youth Network using WIA Youth funds, then worked to include education funds for youth that were disconnected from the education system. The Youth Council was able to make the connection between the need to reengage the high school dropouts and channel them into an accelerated learning environment as opposed to a traditional school environment with strict discipline policies. When they began this work, the four-year graduation rate for this population was 48 percent, and now it's at 61 percent.

Braiding Funds to Help Persons with Disabilities. States also express frustration and confusion about how they can braid vocational rehabilitation, education and training, Medicaid, and other federal funds to support youth and adults with disabilities to secure and keep competitive integrated jobs. In 2015, DOL, ED, SSA and HHS will issue coordinated technical assistance to funding recipients on how disability employment funding and funding for related support services can be braided and encouraging agencies to work together and braid funds to best serve people with disabilities. In addition, HHS and Veterans Health Administration are supporting states to simplify and transform their multiple access points for people with disabilities and older adults who are seeking long-term services and supports, including employment-related supports, regardless of payer, into a single statewide No Wrong Door network.

Myth Busters ED, DOL, HHS, and DOJ, along with the United States Interagency Council on Homelessness, are working together to publish "myth busters" that dispel common myths that exist about barriers to serving disconnected youth. DOL and ED, for example, jointly developed a myth buster that focuses on ways in which Workforce Investment Act funds can be combined with adult education funds to create successful programs. These myth busters will all be published this summer on www.findyouthinfo.gov.

Spreading Innovation across Departments through Collaboration

The Administration, with the leadership of DOL, is working at an unprecedented level to align resources, activities, and strategy to break down silos and develop a job-driven workforce system across federal programs.

Building and Piloting Comprehensive Training Programs into Transportation Careers. The Department of Transportation is kicking off a multi-stage strategy to help the transportation industry better train workers that can meet industry needs. Transportation is collaborating with ED and DOL as well as Jobs for the Future to understand demands for specific types of transportation careers, including regional hot spots for transportation demand. Based on this information, this fall, these partners will convene a meeting with industry leaders, small-to medium-sized enterprises, and top state and local training programs to identify existing challenges and to develop best practices and strategies moving forward. They will then implement a pilot program with five to six state DOTs to demonstrate how comprehensive workforce programs can align funding sources, including DOT highway funding, and forge partnerships to create training programs related to transportation related careers.

Federal Transit Administration's (FTA) Workforce Development Program. FTA's Workforce Development Program has, to date, provided some $10 million in funding to transit agencies and other entities that have implemented innovative solutions to pressing workforce development issues. The funding has been used to upgrade the skills of existing workers and to attract new entrants into the profession, especially those engaged in the maintenance and operation of green technology vehicles and equipment. In FY 2014, FTA hopes to appropriate $7 million for workforce development projects in collaboration with DOL, aimed at creating new Ladders of Opportunity, with special emphasis on training programs, outreach to increase minority and female employment in transit, and training for minority business opportunities. For instance, the Regional Transportation District of Denver, Colorado has leveraged $486,465 in FTA funding to create its Workforce Initiative Now (WIN) program that provides career guidance, job training, coaching and support services for members of the local community, many of them unemployed or veterans, hoping to exercise skilled trades. As a result, WIN has placed some 160 new hires in living wage jobs paying over $16 per hour, and provided a career ladder to professional advancement to over 80 current workers.

The Curb Cuts to the Middle Class Initiative. A cross-agency group, including DOL, ED, DOJ, HHS VA, SSA, the Equal Employment Opportunity Commission, National Council on Disability, and Office of Personnel Management will work together to improve shared mechanisms that will help people with disabilities obtain and retain good jobs. In its pilot year, the group will focus on people with significant disabilities and the affirmative action and nondiscrimination obligations of federal contractors under Section 503 of the Rehabilitation Act. Working together, these agencies will help people with disabilities prepare to qualify for the array of jobs offered by federal contractors; connect federal contractors with jobs to qualified job seekers with disabilities; and provide federal contractors with the tools and resources they need to recruit, retain and promote people with disabilities.

Improving SNAP Employment & Training. DOL and USDA have formed a collaborative partnership to strengthen the relationship between the SNAP E&T program and the WIA workforce development system. The goal is to maximize federal and local resources by integrating or aligning programs and services of the state and local Workforce Investment Boards, the American Job Centers, and SNAP E&T programs to provide SNAP work registrants an opportunity to engage in focused job-driven programs that will increase self-sufficiency and reduce reliance on public assistance, while meeting employer demand for skilled workers. Up to three states or local communities will, on a voluntary basis, test strategies to align services across training, adult education, vocational rehabilitation, and human service programs to improve customer service, optimize employment outcomes, and make more effective use of program funds.

DOL and HUD Resources on Job Training for HUD-Assisted Residents. DOL and HUD recently released a toolkit on successful strategies for creating partnerships between Workforce Investment Boards and public housing authorities. These strategies help public housing residents receive employment and training services through American Job Centers and have created programs that meet the needs of this population. In addition, later this year, HUD will release a $22 million competition for the JOBS-Plus program that will support PHA and workforce partnerships to increase employment opportunities and earnings and savings for HUD-assisted residents.

Creating More Registered Apprenticeship Opportunities for Disconnected Youth. DOL and HUD also released a joint letter encouraging HUD grantees and contractors to partner with YouthBuild and Registered Apprenticeship programs on July 14, 2014.

Collaborating to Help States Create Career Pathways that Create Educational Stepping Stones. ED, DOL, and HHS have coordinated around a common definition and framework of career pathways and in April they issued a request for information (RFI) to solicit recommendations from stakeholders and program heads on how to facilitate career pathways. The agencies received back 146 detailed comments from a range of organizations, including workforce agencies, labor unions, industry associations, and education organizations. An initial analysis of high-level themes from the request for information responses in July 2014 indicated an overarching theme of the comments the agencies received was the importance of giving States and localities greater flexibility in the administration of education, training, and human services programs through waivers or other means. The benefits of establishing common performance measures across education, training, and human services programs was another repeated theme, as was the necessity of interagency partnerships. In the view of many commenters, federal policy should continue to set clear expectations for cross-agency collaboration as well as continue to offer technical assistance to states to help facilitate career pathway partnerships. This initial analysis will be used to inform strategic technical assistance and investments for career pathways to solicit recommendations from stakeholders and program heads on how to facilitate career pathways. A more detailed and final analysis of the RFI responses will be issued in fall 2014. In September 2014 HHS, DOL, and ED, in collaboration with DOT and the Department of Energy, will be convening a National Dialogue on career pathways. The meeting will bring together state administrators of the federal programs, researchers, and representatives from the philanthropic community.

Ladders of Opportunity Initiative. DOT, DOL, and ED are working together to invest in projects that improve the work-related mobility of Americans with transportation disadvantages, including those with disabilities and those of lower income. DOT recently announced the availability of more than $100 million in grants that focus on enhancing accessibility to work and supporting local partnerships from the transit, workforce development, and education communities. The agencies are continuing discussions to enhance career pathways in the transportation sector for these groups.

Manufacturing Extension Partnership. DOC's Manufacturing Extension Partnership and DOL will work together on a series of webinars and joint outreach to promote closer collaboration between workforce boards and MEP centers in efforts such as Registered Apprenticeships, layoff aversion, sector strategies, skills information, and others. Similarly, MEP has begun discussions with ED about similar joint outreach between MEP centers and community colleges to raise awareness about collaborative opportunities and to spotlight best practices where partnerships are already working very well together. For example, MEP co-hosted a webinar for MEP centers on 21st century apprenticeships with DOL's Office of Apprenticeship on July 16th. MEP is also in discussions with ED's Office of Career, Technical, and Adult Education regarding career pathways and community colleges and potential partnerships with MEP, with potential next steps identified by the end of the summer.

Layoff Aversion

Over the past several years, the California Manufacturing Technology Consulting ("CMTC," a CA MEP center) has worked collaboratively with multiple local Workforce Investment Boards and other partners to implement business retention and layoff aversion programs focused on the region's manufacturing sector. Over the course of the effort, 198 manufacturers were engaged and 2,654 jobs were created or retained and $108 million in new and retained sales were realized (source: MEP client survey.) For example, Accurate Dial is a client 65-year-old company in Glendale, CA with three generations of workers in their 22-person company. However, they had suffered a 25 percent reduction in sales, and many workers were put in jeopardy. CMTC conducted an in-depth analysis for their business and implemented lean manufacturing principles, IS9001 certification for quality, and today they are acquiring new contracts and were able to retain 10 jobs that were targeted for possible layoff.

3 The Opportunity Ahead: A Call to Action for American Skills and Jobs

To achieve our goal of training many more Americans with the in-demand skills that employers need and matching them to good jobs that need to be filled right now, we must replicate the individual beacons of success identified over the past 180 days, moving beyond single-case partnerships to industry-wide partnerships and scalable models. And the only way to get there is working together.

The changes outlined in this report for federal employment and training programs will ensure that $17 billion in federal workforce spending each year is more job-driven and effective, but given the size and scale of the challenges we face, that alone is not enough. That is why we are working to mobilize industry, education, innovators and communities across the country to devise, replicate, and scale up solutions to enable ordinary Americans to find pathways to good jobs and careers, to mobilize employers to recruit and hire the skilled workers they need to compete, and to mobilize American communities to attract business investment and create jobs by building skilled workforces.

3.1 FIELDING A FULL TEAM: GETTING LONG-TERM UNEMPLOYED AMERICANS BACK TO WORK

As the economy improves, and even in an expansionary job market, it is critical that certain groups of Americans that have job-ready skills are not left behind. A complex labor market can make it difficult for individuals to get on the right pathways, even if they possess needed skills. Arbitrary education and training requirements for jobs and employer hiring screens based on factors other than skills for the job can make it harder for people to get jobs.

In January, the President called attention to one group being left behind: the long-term unemployed. Even with a strengthening job market and growing economy, the country continues to face a challenge of long-term unemployment. In June, there were 3.1 million long-term unemployed individuals, making up 32.8 percent of all the unemployed. The long-term unemployed are a diverse group of workers. Unlike in other recessions, the long-term unemployed are not the most disadvantaged workers. Today, the long-term unemployed are slightly *more* educated on average than their recently unemployed peers: 27 percent of the long-term unemployed have post-secondary credentials, compared to 24.5 percent of the short-term unemployed.[27] Although older workers are disproportionately counted among the long-term unemployed, 70 percent of the long-term unemployed are younger than 50.[28] In addition, the long-term unemployed are not concentrated among any particular industry and are comparable to the short-term unemployed.

---

[27] Internal calculations based on *Bureau of Labor Statistics* data.
[28] Internal calculations based on *Bureau of Labor Statistics* data.

There is also new evidence since January that the long-term unemployed have similar job performance to others. As reported by Bloomberg in April, Evolv used data on entry-level call center agents from six employers in about 90 U.S. locations – a pool of about 20,000 employees – and found that those who had been long-term unemployed had similar outcomes to recently unemployed individuals on measures of performance like productivity, customer satisfaction, and supervisor evaluations.[29]

Evolv

San Francisco-based Evolv is helping several of the largest companies who have signed Obama's pledge to systematically remove bias from their hiring and workforce management practices, and in turn put a measurable dent in the job placement challenge faced by so many of the nation's long-term unemployed. By utilizing big data and predictive analytics to analyze millions of employees every day, Evolv helps companies hire and manage workforces more fairly, effectively and productively. Evolv's insights have surprised and challenged some of the most widely held (and often biased) beliefs around hiring and workplace management.

For example, Evolv's data has proven that the long-term unemployed perform no worse than those without extended jobless spells, that prior work experience and even education are not predictive of job performance in some roles, and that applicants with a history of "job hopping" are not bad hires.

Some of the 300 companies that signed Obama's pledge – including **AT&T, Xerox, and Kelly Services** – have implemented Evolv's technology to improve their hiring practices, combat discrimination and deliver better performance. In the case of Xerox, Evolv data found that hiring based on prior work experience in a similar role was not predictive of success. In changing their hiring criteria, Xerox opened up new doors for candidates who would never have gotten to interview based upon their resume. This, along with other data insights, helped Xerox hire more people who are better suited to their jobs, perform better and stay longer - reducing attrition rates by 20 percent.

Big data and predictive analytics when applied to the workforce have the potential to do enormous good for the private sector. While algorithms will never replace humans, using science and evidence-based data to make better hiring and management decisions will only improve the lives and future opportunities for the American workforce.

Despite these similarities, the long-term unemployed face challenges in the labor market because of their long-term unemployment. Multiple studies have shown that the long-term unemployed are less likely to be called back for interviews than the short-term unemployed, even with identical resumes. To land an interview, a long-term unemployed individual must apply to 3.5 times as many jobs as a recently unemployed individual. Applicants unemployed for seven months need to send an average of 35 resumes to online job postings to receive just one interview, compared to just 10 resumes per interview for those unemployed for only one month.[30]

In January, the President hosted a White House summit on long-term unemployment organized around three objectives that, when combined, will help make sure Americans that are ready to work can find jobs.

---

[29] Aki Ito, "Long-Term Unemployed Make for Just as Strong Hires: Study," *Bloomberg* (April 2014).
[30] Rand Ghayad, "The Jobless Trap," *Job Market Paper*, Working Paper (2013).

1. Engaging Employers in Best Practices for Hiring and Recruiting the Long-Term Unemployed. The Administration engaged with America's leading businesses to develop best practices for hiring and recruiting the long-term unemployed to ensure that these candidates receive a fair shot during the hiring process. Over 80 of the nation's largest businesses have signed on, including 20 members of the Fortune 50 and over 45 members of the Fortune 200, as well as over 200 small- and medium-sized businesses.

2. Encouraging Regional Collaboration to Get the Long-Term Unemployed Back to Work. The Administration launched a $150 Million Ready to Work Partnership grant to support and scale innovative partnerships among employers and non-profits in states and cities across the country that are helping to prepare and place the long-term unemployed into good jobs.

3. Ensuring Federal Policies Support Hiring of the Long-Term Unemployed. The President used his executive authority to sign a Presidential Memorandum to make sure that individuals who are unemployed or have faced financial difficulties through no fault of their own receive fair treatment and consideration for employment by federal agencies.

Since January, long-term unemployment has declined by 500,000 individuals. This drop has accounted for over 70 percent of the overall drop in unemployment. The long-term unemployment rate also fell faster over the last six months than the previous six months. Over the first half of 2014, the long-term unemployment rate came down 0.5 p.p., including a 0.2 p.p. decline in June.[31]

Though we have seen progress, the long-term unemployment rate remains well above its 2001 through 2007 average of 1.0 percent.[32] The strategies the President prioritized at the White House summit are still critical to continue and accelerate the rate of long-term unemployed who find jobs.

Today, the White House is able to announce progress on the President's initiatives.

Spreading Best Practices on Hiring the Long-Term Unemployed and Expanding Regional Partnerships

Businesses that signed onto the White House Best Practices are taking the request to change their recruiting and hiring practices seriously. The White House conducted a survey of businesses signing onto the White House Best Practices on Recruiting and Hiring the Long-Term Unemployed in June. Based on this survey, Best Practices are viewed as effective by an overwhelming majority of businesses and have led to hiring of the long-term unemployed. The survey, which was conducted anonymously, found that the most effective best practice in generating hires is engaging with local and regional entities. Some survey respondents volunteered to have their stories shared and their experiences with the Best Practices are in gray box below.

Long-Term Unemployment Playbooks. As part of their commitment to enhance employment opportunities among American workers and address the challenges the long-term unemployed typically face in finding employment, Deloitte and the Rockefeller Foundation are working together to create playbooks that can be used by employers and long-term unemployed job seekers to return a

---

[31] Internal calculations based on *Bureau of Labor Statistics* data.
[32] *Bureau of Labor Statistics.*

greater number of job seekers to the workforce. Based on interviews with employers, job seekers, and employment partners across the United States, the playbooks are an exciting next step following on the heels of the White House-led Best Practices for Recruiting and Hiring the Long-Term Unemployed. The employer playbook will provide tactical tools to help employers operationalize the Best Practices and tap into the full potential of the long-term unemployed population. The job seeker playbook will be designed specifically for the long-term unemployed, providing them with targeted resources and recommendations to improve their job searching process. Before release, they will engage several cities in a pilot to deploy the playbooks.

Demand-Driven Guide to Expand and Improve Regional Partnerships. In response to requests for sharing best practices to support replication of its demand-driven model, Skills for Chicagoland's Future is finalizing an online playbook of core principles and materials that organizations in locations across the country can use in implementing a demand-driven model. A sneak preview of the demand-driven model playbook can be found online now at www.SCFplaybook.com. The playbook serves as a blueprint for organizations interested in creating, transforming into or incubating a demand-driven business intermediary as well as tools to operate a demand-driven model. The playbook was made possible by support from the Aspen Institute's Skills for America's Future. Skills for Chicagoland's Future has used this model to hire almost 1,000 people since launching in 2012, and 70 percent of those individuals have been long-term unemployed, showing how a demand-driven model can be effective at both meeting business needs and helping disadvantaged groups.

Networking Tools for the Long-Term Unemployed. As a part of the White House's initiative on long-term unemployment, LinkedIn made a commitment to work with winners of the Ready to Work Partnership grants. They committed to work with a select number of grantees to help them identify, connect, and support the long-term unemployed in their regions. The grants will be awarded in the fall, but in the meantime, LinkedIn has already begun partnering with a state to offer LinkedIn networking tools to the long-term unemployed.

The Ready to Work Partnership grants announced in January generated a great deal of interest, with over 150 applications. In the process of applying for these grants many organizations like San Francisco JVS (below) have learned more about the long-term unemployed populations in their area and are developing strategies to address these needs. Additionally, the Department of Labor was able to make $155 million available for grants through its Dislocated Worker National Reserve and some of these grants are aimed at addressing long-term unemployment. For example, Nevada will help expand the Platform to Employment model to help the long-term unemployed get back to work. Vermont will expand the Vermont HITEC model into the state's American Job Centers to serve long-term unemployed workers; HITEC is an innovative accelerated training and work-based learning model to help unemployed individuals obtain jobs in health care information technology. New Hampshire also received funds to expand its on-the-job training program that benefits the long-term unemployed.

Several governors have made long-term unemployment a priority as well. Governor Inslee of Washington announced grants for returning the long-term unemployed to work in May.[33] In January,

---

[33] "Gov. Inslee announces grant award to return long-term unemployed to work," *Employment Security Department Washington State* (May 2014).

Governor Malloy of Connecticut announced his support for a $3.6 million legislative package, which included the creation of a statewide Platform 2 Employment program serving 500 long-term unemployed Connecticut residents. With broad support from both sides of the aisle, the General Assembly's budget, which passed in May, included the Governor's recommendation.[34]

Aetna

Aetna, one of the nation's leading diversified health care benefits companies, joined the White House Best Practices pledge in January. Since that time, Aetna formed a relationship with Skills for Chicagoland's Future Talent, one of the organizations highlighted during the White House's events on long-term unemployment. The primary objective of their joint program was to assist the unemployed in finding jobs and to ensure these individuals were properly trained to maximize their success once hired.

Their relationship with the organization was formed a few short months ago with a goal to hire 10 people for Aetna's Chicago office. Skills for Chicagoland's Future Talent screened, interviewed and presented Aetna with 20 highly qualified candidates to be considered for 10 open roles. Aetna was extremely impressed with the caliber and overall quality of the candidates. Aetna hired 10 new employees from that group of candidates on June 23rd. To date, Aetna is pleased to report that all are successful.

Frontier Communications

Frontier Communications Corporation is America's largest communications company, providing broadband, voice, and television products and services to rural areas and small and medium-sized communities in 27 states.

Frontier has formally committed to giving the long-term unemployed a better chance at a good job by adopting best practices on recruiting and hiring. However, years before its CEO signed the Best Practices Pledge, Frontier was alert to eliminating hiring screens, such as credit checks, that could inadvertently disadvantage the long-term unemployed. Removing the credit checks had no negative effect, a fact the company recently proved by reviewing hires who would have been "screened out" had a credit check policy been in place. Looking at 30 hires, 95 percent of those hired would have failed a credit check. This talent would have been lost due to a screen with no bearing on a position's job qualifications or the applicant's performance. The ripple effect of a "do not hire" decision significantly and negatively affects an applicant's (and his/her family's) housing, health insurance, self-respect, and more. Frontier is a better company for having a talented and dedicated new employee.

Since signing the Best Practices Pledge, Frontier has implemented other steps to make their hiring process more accessible and user-friendly. For example, video interviewing is now common (in person interviews are an option) and has made the hiring process more accessible to those with physical challenges. Video interviews are especially helpful for customer service jobs, allowing the off-site interviewer/hiring manager to appreciate "soft" competencies not apparent from a resume. Interviews with applicants having high levels of these competencies can result in job offers, demonstrating that a resume showing wide gaps in employment is not an indicator of a candidate's overall abilities. The success of video interviewing has expanded hiring pools; hiring managers see it as a positive development and it is appreciated by applicants who might not be able to travel easily, for whatever reason, to an interview site.

Frontier Communications is now a member of Platform to Employment, a nationally-recognized program to help long-term unemployed workers get back to work. The Company plans to use Platform to Employment for more hires in 2014. In addition, in June 2014, Frontier's Vice President of Talent Acquisition and Development, was appointed to the board of the WorkPlace

MetLife

MetLife has joined an extensive list of U.S. companies participating in the White House's Long-Term Unemployment Initiative. In support of the initiative, MetLife is undertaking efforts to promote the hiring of the long-term unemployed. This has included educating its recruiters about the issue and soliciting their feedback on ways to improve on hiring and outreach efforts that will assist with recruiting the long-term unemployed.

MetLife is also partnering with local intermediary organizations in Warwick, Rhode Island and Raleigh, North Carolina that support the hiring of the long-term unemployed. In Warwick, MetLife is working with a non-profit organization that provides job seekers with pre-employment preparation and training programs and connects job seekers to employers. In Raleigh, MetLife is working with Wake Technical Community College which has applied for one of the Ready to Work grants to train the long-term unemployed and veterans in cybersecurity.

---

[34] "Governor Malloy Announces Programs for Long-Term Unemployed," *Connecticut Department of Labor* (February 2014).

As these efforts continue, it remains of vital importance to provide support to the long-term unemployed as they continue their job search. As the President noted on July 10th in a speech in Austin, the long-term unemployed, like the woman who introduced him, "have paid taxes all their lives and never depended on anything and just needed a little help to get over a hump."

According to DOL, since the expiration of the Emergency Unemployment Compensation program at the end of 2013, 1.3 million people were immediately cut off benefits, and another 1.6 million people exhausted their regular unemployment insurance without the ability to transition onto emergency benefits. Another 1.48 million people are expected to exhaust unemployment benefits before the end of the year. Emergency unemployment insurance provides a crucial financial bridge for those actively seeking employment, while connecting the long-term unemployed to the labor market.

Update on Workforce Partnerships Serving the Long-Term Unemployed

Platform 2 Employment

Platform 2 Employment provides workshops and personal counseling while placing participants in subsidized work experiences in fields for which they are qualified. Since the long-term unemployment event at the White House, Platform 2 Employment has expanded to two additional cities—San Francisco and Tampa. Platform 2 Employment has also benefited from a Job-Driven National Emergency Grant awarded in June to Nevada, where they will be opening sites in Reno and Las Vegas. They have also been asked to partner with several cities to expand as a part of Ready to Work Partnership grant proposals. P2E has broadened its partnerships, now working with vocational rehabilitation agencies to expand the number of persons with disabilities in their employment and training programs.

San Francisco Jewish Vocational Service (SF JVS)

San Francisco Jewish Vocational Services provides reemployment and training to many long-term unemployed, and they attended the White House Summit on Long-Term Unemployment. Since the summit they have seen their placements of the long-term unemployed increase by 13 percent. They believe this was due to increased awareness among businesses of the challenges facing the long-term unemployed thanks to the President's highlighting of the issue. San Francisco JVS applied for DOL's Ready to Work grants, and this provided an impetus to do a deep-dive into the long-term unemployment problem, including surveys of individuals and employers, to develop program models that will better suit their needs.

Skills for Chicagoland's Future

Skills for Chicagoland's Future works with employers through a demand-driven model to help place the unemployed into their companies and coordinates among non-profits to find unemployed workers looking for jobs. When the White House held the long-term unemployment event on January 31st, Skills for Chicagoland's Future had hired over 600 people since launching in 2012 and over 70 percent of them were long-term unemployed. Since the summit, SFC has been able to 370 more hires due to a higher level of interest from employer partners including new partners like Aetna (see box above.). SCF is on track to place 670 jobseekers in jobs in 2014, up from the 540 placed in 2013.

3.2 UPSKILLING AMERICA: FROM DEAD-END JOBS TO MIDDLE CLASS CAREER PATHWAYS

Working Hard, But Not Getting Ahead: The Opportunity Gap For Lower-Skilled Workers

The opportunity

24 million employed adults have low literacy skills.

Wages increase by **28 percent** with a one-standard deviation increase in numeracy

$300K lifetime ROI for apprentices

Lower-skilled workers make up a significant part of the U.S. adult labor force. According to the OECD's 2013 Program for the International Assessment of Adult Competencies (PIAAC) study of basic skills, approximately 36 million U.S. adults between the ages of 16 and 65 have low literacy skills, and 62 million, or 30 percent, have low numeracy skills.[35] These numbers are higher among unemployed workers: 23 percent of unemployed adults have low literacy skills, and 42 percent of unemployed adults have low numeracy skills.

At the same time, 24 million low literacy adults – nearly two-thirds of the total – are working, and the skills deficiencies they face often make it difficult to be promoted into jobs at higher wages, no matter how motivated and reliable they may be. Among employed adults in the bottom 40 percent of monthly earnings, a quarter has low literacy skills and 37 percent have low numeracy skills, compared with 6 percent and 9 percent in the top quintile, respectively.[36]

Relative to the 36 million adults with severe deficits in workforce literacy, the current federally-funded adult education system reaches fewer than 2 million adults each year.[37] Unsurprisingly, lower-skilled workers and job seekers include many individuals traditionally underserved by training programs, including 12.4 million adults who do not speak English well or at all, some adults with disabilities or chronic health issues, and many individuals re-entering society from incarceration.[38]

This gap presents an enormous opportunity. Adults' skills strongly affect their social mobility:

Who are the lower skilled in America?

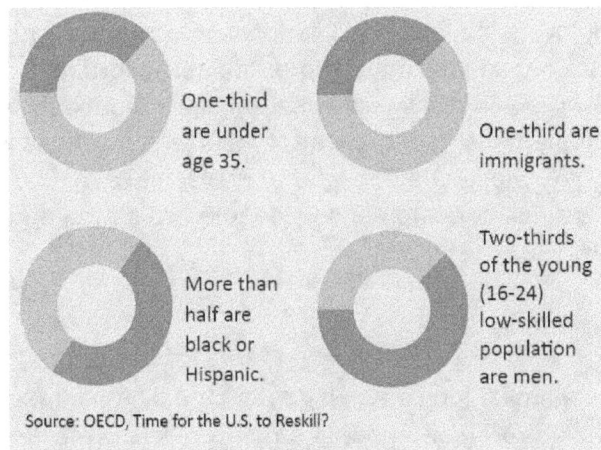

One-third are under age 35.

One-third are immigrants.

More than half are black or Hispanic.

Two-thirds of the young (16-24) low-skilled population are men.

Source: OECD, Time for the U.S. to Reskill?

the economic payoff to individuals with higher skills is greater in the United States than in almost any other OECD country. An OECD study found that a one-standard-deviation increase in numeracy skills is associated with a 28 percent wage increase among prime-age workers.[39] Skill levels are also a

---

[35] Individual was at or below level 1 on the PIAAC scale.

[36] Internal calculations based on OECD, *Program for the International Assessment of Adult Competencies* (2013).

[37] "Adult Education Basic Grant Program Factsheet," *Department of Education Office of Career, Technical, and Adult Education* (June 2014).

[38] Data from *U.S. Census*.

[39] Eric A. Hanushek, et al., "Return to Skills Around the World: Evidence from PIACC," *OECD Education Working Paper 101* (2013).

concern for local, regional, and national economies. Among industrialized nations, higher levels of adult skills have higher productivity and substantially higher long-term economic growth. In the United States, states with better-educated workforces have higher economic growth and higher wages.[40] And skills development is a concern for businesses. In a 2012 McKinsey survey, 36 percent of employers reported that a lack of employee skills caused "significant problems in terms of cost, quality, and time," bolstering the business case for employers to invest in upgrading the skills of their front-line employees.[41]

There is evidence that education and training programs offered through the workplace can benefit both workers and employers. For example, a quasi-experimental evaluation of a workplace literacy program for low-wage manufacturing workers found that average wage growth for participants was higher than that for non-participants and that participants were more likely to apply for and to receive promotions than comparable non-participants.[42] A random assignment study of workplace literacy programs conducted in late 1990s also found positive impacts of literacy programs on worker outcomes, including improved skills, attendance, and job performance; higher receipt of job benefits; and development of new career plans.[43]

Examples of Job-Driven Training and Industry Career Pathways for Upward Mobility

On-Ramps in Retail

Nearly 20 percent of workers employed in the retail industry are lower-skilled, an industry which has been seen by some as lacking career potential.[44] However, moving up to retail supervisor roles can provide a meaningful "skills on-ramp" to jobs across industries and occupations. The skills employees build in retail supervisor jobs have particularly strong relevance to higher-paid sales and customer service management roles. According to data collected by Burning Glass, over 28 percent of workers in retail supervisor roles without bachelor's degrees transition to sales and customer care management. These are attainable jobs for these workers, because 47 percent of them do not require bachelor's degrees. They also offer middle-class wages; the average advertised annual salary for a sales or customer service role two career steps away from a retail supervisor position is $56,392.[45]

On-Ramps in IT

A range of IT jobs are in high demand. IT jobs are unusual in that, more than any other occupational field, a growing number of employers treat relevant skill and competency as a sufficient qualification

---

[40] Eric A. Hanushek and Ludger Woessman, "How Much Do Educational Outcomes Matter in OECD Countries?" Working Paper 16515, *NBER* (November 2010).

[41] Mona Mourshed, Diana Farrell, and Dominic Barton, "Education to Employment: Designing a System that Works," *McKinsey Center for Government* (2013).

[42] A. Krueger and C. Rouse, "New Evidence on Workplace Education Working Paper 4831," *National Bureau of Economic Research* (1994).

[43] M.T. Moore, D. Myers, and T. Silva, "Addressing Literacy Needs at Work: Implementation and Impact of Workplace Literacy Programs: Final Report of national evaluation of NWLP partnerships," (1998).

[44] "Program for the International Assessment of Adult Competencies," *OECD* (2013).

[45] "Retail Career Ladders," *Burning Glass Technologies* (unpublished).

for employment, making many well-paying IT jobs accessible to individuals without traditional educational credentials. In IT, if you demonstrate that you can do the job, you often can get the job. IT jobs made up 15 percent of middle-skill job postings in a 2013 Burning Glass analysis.[46] In an analysis of the Houston metropolitan statistical area, computer user support specialists – a high number of which are sub-bachelor's degree positions – commanded the second-highest median wages of any "bachelor's degree not required" occupations, behind nurses. Network and systems administration roles present a particularly strong opportunity to upskill workers without a formal bachelor's degree. In 2013, there were over 12,000 postings for entry-level job postings in network and systems administration that did not require a bachelor's degree – 38 percent of total job postings in the occupation.[47]

Critically, IT support roles can serve as on-ramps to higher-skill jobs that offer workers higher salaries. In the Houston area, 100 percent of computer retail sales and support roles, and 97 percent of PC repair roles, were available to workers without bachelor's degrees. These positions serve as ramps to higher-wage positions in advanced computer support, network support, and helpdesk management. From computer retail sales and PC repair roles, acquiring credentials such as Microsoft Certified Solutions Expert, Cisco Certified Network Associate, Security+, Network+, and A+ can signal that workers have the skills to work in entry-level computer support. From there, acquiring credentials such as Microsoft Certified Professional and Cisco Certified Network Associate, as well as skills such as SQL, WAN, and TCP/IP can position individuals to work in advanced computer support and network support.[48]

Wadhwani Foundation "Race to a Job"

In 2012, the Wadhwani Foundation launched the "Race to a Job" (RTAJ) initiative. The mission of RTAJ is to enhance student employability while reducing learning times and costs and improving completion. Wadhwani is pioneering a learner-centric massively open online system delivered in a hybrid model that scales existing successful workforce development programs in collaboration with community colleges, community-based organizations, training unions and industry partners. Wadhwani rolled out two pilot partnerships in 2013. Anne Arundel Community College (AACC), a part of the National STEM Consortium, is working with Wadhwani to transform their Cyber Technology Certificate program designed to prepare entry-level cyber technology workers for career pathways in IT. The AACC student profile is immensely diverse and the focus is on job seekers with little prior education; industry certifications granted include CompTIA (A+, Security+, Net+) and Cisco (CCNA). Wadhwani is also partnering with the Borough of Manhattan Community College of City University of New York & 1199 SEIU Training and Upgrading Fund in New York for digitization of their Medical Assistant Specialist curriculum with an aim to upgrade skills and help workers gain stackable credentials. Other collaborators include New York City Small Business Services, Community Health Care Association of New York State, and the New York Alliance for Careers in Health care.

---

[46] "Identifying High Value Middle-Skill Career Targets," *Burning Glass Technologies* (2014).
[47] "Identifying High Value Middle-Skill Career Targets," *Burning Glass Technologies* (2014).
[48] "Identifying High Value Middle-Skill Career Targets," *Burning Glass Technologies* (2014).

Modernizing Apprenticeships and On-the-Job Training to Upskill Workers

On-the-job training and apprenticeships are critical strategies for skill development for adult learners who often lack the time and money to invest in traditional educational programs and degrees. Apprenticeships have always been a part of the American training system, but for too long we have underinvested in the infrastructure to support employers and training organizations to start and expand apprenticeship programs. Where apprenticeships are working – often in collaboration with skilled trades unions – employers can help to expand them; where new models of apprenticeship are relevant for new occupations and industries, our policies should encourage industry and employers to adapt and adopt them. Moreover, in 2014, employers can use apprenticeships to "upskill" and credential and retain their current workers in a more expansive approach to on-the-job training.

In partnership with employers, labor unions, training organizations, and state and local officials across the country, the Administration is taking strides to dramatically increase the opportunity for American workers and employers to benefit from apprenticeships and on-the-job training.

Modernizing and Expanding the Office of Apprenticeship. Building off a series of industry roundtables held across the country, DOL will increase its Office of Apprenticeship's capabilities to partner with employers on creating and expanding apprenticeships in multiple ways. In six regions across the country, the Office of Apprenticeship will add additional staff and launch new industry-focused technical assistance efforts to help employers start or expand apprenticeship programs. DOL will also begin efforts to provide new electronic tools to support employers while streamlining the registration process for apprenticeship programs, with a new, electronic registration process that should reduce the time required for registration, while maintaining a high bar for program quality.

SEIU Leadership in Apprenticeships

Washington will need to train approximately 440,000 home care workers by 2030 to meet growing demand as Baby Boomers age. The SEIU Health care NW Training Partnership (Training Partnership) aims to work to fill this need. In total, the Training Partnership trains 40,000 students each year in Washington, making it the largest home care workforce training provider in the nation. The Training Partnership has also piloted the country's first DOL Registered Apprenticeship program for home care aides. The one-year apprenticeship program aims to help home care aides obtain state certification and raise the quality and composition of home care workers. In April, the White House highlighted the Training Partnership's plans to partner with several employers of home care workers in Washington – including government and private companies such as ResCare and Addus – and its stated goal of expanding its apprenticeship program for home care workers over the next five years from 300 to 3,000 apprentices per year. Over the next few months, the Aspen Institute, with support from the Ford Foundation and SkillUp Washington, will conduct a study of the Training Partnership's approach to better understand the impact of the organization's training on the state's home care workforce and home care consumers.

Reducing Barriers to Individuals Pursuing Apprenticeships. Employers who offer apprenticeships can find it difficult to attract a diverse group of apprentice candidates to expand their programs. In June, DOL awarded three new apprenticeship assistance centers with grants to support employers looking to recruit more women into apprenticeship. With women only making up 7 percent of apprentices, they represent an untapped source of skills and talent for employers seeking a skilled workforce. The

Office of Apprenticeship is also planning to update its regulations to enhance opportunities for women, minorities, and individuals with disabilities in apprenticeship.

Laying the Groundwork for Fall Apprenticeship Competition. In partnership with a range of national organizations, Skills for America's Future will undertake an outreach and capacity-building program for prospective applicants and their employer partners to the forthcoming grant solicitation on the expansion of the country's apprenticeship opportunities. This outreach will include the development of webinars and resource materials to provide an overview to apprenticeship models, best practice examples of apprenticeships, and tools for developing and growing apprenticeship programs.

Connecting Apprentices with College Credit. The Registered Apprenticeship College Consortium (RACC), a partnership among community colleges, national accreditors, employers, and major apprenticeship sponsors, is making it possible for apprentices to earn college credits for their apprenticeship training that will transfer to any community college in the consortium they attend. Founding members include large state systems like Ohio and Wisconsin. Since it was launched in April by the Vice President, 14 colleges, four national Registered Apprenticeship sponsors with 575 affiliated local programs, and three other state-wide community college systems have applied to join the consortium.

Employer Investment in Skills and Training

Most training in the United States occurs at the workplace: over a quarter of all workers report that they receive some formal job training from their employers,[49] and about 70 percent of firms indicate they offer some type of training to employees.[50] The vast majority of these resources are invested in professional development and training for more highly skilled employees. The PIAAC Survey of Adult Skills found that the participation rate in job-related education and training in the United States in 2012 ranged from 21 percent for adults with the lowest level literacy skills to 69 percent for

McDonald's English Under the Arches Example

McDonald's offers employees the English Under the Arches program (EUA), a nationally-recognized workplace ELL program that provides English language instruction using a combination of technology and in-person instruction. McDonald's developed the program after realizing that many staff members held great potential for workplace advancement yet lacked the language skills to fully compete for the positions. Begun through a series of pilots in 2007, EUA is designed for McDonald's managers and manager trainees. Individual franchise owners select managers and manager trainees to participate in the program, pay their tuition, and provide paid work time for the employees to attend classes while at work. Classes are held during work time in McDonald's restaurants (five hours per week), and employees connect with other student-employees and the teacher in real time in a "virtual classroom." allowing employees to gain the language skills they need to advance without losing work or transportation time. In addition to the virtual classes, students learn through face-to-face classes and on-the-job practice. The program has had over 2,500 participants since 2008, has 91 percent course completion, 88 percent employee retention one year after graduation, 84 percent two years after graduation, and 73 percent three and four years after graduation. Over 95 percent of participants saw their wages increase.

---

[49] Robert I. Lerman, Signe-Mary McKernan and Stephanie Riegg, "The Scope of Employer-Provided Training in the United States: Who, What, Where, and How Much?" *Job Training Policy in the United States* (2004).
[50] Robert I. Lerman, Signe-Mary McKernan and Stephanie Riegg, "The Scope of Employer-Provided Training in the United States: Who, What, Where, and How Much?" *Job Training Policy in the United States* (2004).

adults with the highest level literacy skills.[51]

The good news is that companies are investing in new ways to train their employees, and we must work to ensure entry level and lower-skilled workers are able to reap the benefits of these investments. In a 2013 Accenture survey, 72 percent of executives identified training as one of the top ways for employees to develop new skills. At the same time, only 52 percent of workers employed by the companies surveyed currently receive company-provided, formal training – but 51 percent of companies expect to increase investments in training over the next two years, and 35 percent of executives whose companies are facing skills shortages acknowledge that they have not invested enough in training in the past.[52] Developing cost-effective job-driven models for employers to upskill their entry-level and lower-skilled employees can widen career opportunities.

The English Works commitment is an example of what an upskilling compact might look like. The Massachusetts Immigrant and Refugee Coalition, in partnership with the National Partnership for New Americans and in coordination with relevant federal agencies including the Department of Education, has committed to identifying, training and assisting five states or metropolitan regions with high concentrations or rapid growth in immigrant and refugee families in the next year with the replication and scaling of the English Works Campaign. This campaign is one successful model, and has called upon business, labor, community, and government leaders to dedicate the needed public and private resources to create a sustainable, high-quality English language learning system that addresses the needs and interests of immigrant workers and their employers. The commitment entails replicating this campaign by identifying five additional states and regions, training these states and regions, coaching the creation and implementation of business-education partnerships, sharing best practices of these public-private partnerships, and creating a national learning community.

> **Northrop Grumman "Pay for Skills"**
>
> Northrop Grumman created a recruitment program called "Pay for Skills," aimed at grooming entry-level workers for higher-level positions and growing talent from within. Pay for Skills was launched in conjunction with an apprenticeship program for high school graduates. Roughly 2,000 employees participate in the program each month, and Northrop Grumman has explicitly recognized the importance of non-traditional learning: "for every professional who comes out of a four-year university, arguably you need 10, 12 or 15 technicians or support people to support that one four-year professional." Within a few years of starting the program in 2001, entry-level attrition rate in the first year of employment plunged from over 20 percent to the single digits.

The Administration is committed to working closely with leading employers, labor unions, training organizations, and state and local officials across the country to identify these best practice strategies, to learn what policies and tools can facilitate investments in job skills that pay dividends for employers and greatly increase opportunities for upward mobility among American workers.

Working with Unions and Labor-Management Partnerships to Expand Quality Training Programs to Provide Pathways to Middle-Class Jobs. In partnership with ED, over 45 unions and labor management organizations have pledged to expand access to their training programs, to share best practices on effective workforce and career pathway programs, and to expand opportunities for

---

[51] *"Survey of Adult Skills," The Organization for Economic Co-operation and Development* (2013).
"2013 Skills and Employment Trends Survey: Perspectives on Training," *Accenture* (October 2013).

women to improve their foundational skills to access higher-wage occupations in construction, transportation, health care, and manufacturing. This collaboration represents partnerships with almost 8,000 employers and will provide unprecedented access to educational and training opportunities as well as supportive services necessary for women and working families to be successful.

Data-Driven Approach to Helping Entry-Level Workers Progress up the Career Ladder. In support of the White House initiative to help lower-wage workers gain skills to advance to higher paying jobs, Burning Glass Technologies will support a coalition of employers in selected industries and other partners with data and analytics on how lower-wage American workers can progress from job to job, highlighting specific skills they need to take the next steps along their career pathways. These career pathway roadmaps will help prioritize the education and training content that committed employers can make available to invest in the career and wage progression of their entry level workers.

Helping States Create Career Pathway Systems for Workers of all Skill Levels. The career pathway model is a tool to help states organize the myriad of education, training, and work-based career preparation options available to students, workers, and job seekers along a modular system of demand-driven post-secondary and industry-recognized credentials that build upon each other. The goal is to create a more efficient pipeline whereby an individual can navigate their education and training choices with greater clarity on the relative market value of skills before they make significant investments of their time or resources. ED will launch the Career Pathways Exchange, an online information dissemination service that will give all states and interested stakeholders access to resources and guidance to develop, expand, and strengthen their career pathways systems. ED will work with 14 states to provide intensive, customized technical assistance, tools, and coaching to make their education and training systems easier to navigate. By implementing a comprehensive assessment tool and new maturity model common to each initiative, each participating state will be able to determine its own implementation status and needs, which will be met through customized technical assistance efforts offered jointly through DOL, ED, and HHS. Additionally, ED is committing to invest in up to 10 states to further integrate career and technical education (CTE) into broader career pathways system development at the state and local level.

Year of Engagement Around Foundation Skills. To inform a national response to the issue of so many Americans needing stronger math and literacy foundational skills, ED embarked on almost a full year of study and engagement with key stakeholders. ED will be releasing a plan in late summer that includes specific strategies to increase access to foundation skills. The plan, "Making Skills Everyone's Business," aims to expand opportunities for adults to assess, improve, and use their foundational skills and proposes to increase the number of adults that will have such opportunities by three million.

Encouraging Greater Employer-Community College Engagement. As a complement to federal efforts to develop job-driven workforce development practices, Skills for America's Future will survey state policy-makers to explore how state policies can encourage and support community college engagement of employers. SAF will develop a policy-maker's guide to support state officials and community college leaders in working closely with employers to foster better outcomes for job seekers. SAF will also work directly with community colleges to develop tools and practices for assessing their current employer engagement and to suggest strategies for expand partnerships with employers to support the implementation of job-driven employment practices.

Universal Availability of Low-Cost Online Learning Tools

In recent years there has been an explosion of massive open online courses (MOOCs), by which high-quality college courses have become available to the masses. This explosion has mostly been driven by users who are already highly educated, many of whom have bachelor's or master's degrees. These users are generally accessing the online content to refresh subjects that they have previously studied or to learn a little about new topics they are considering pursuing. There is a huge opportunity to develop online content that could be used to help upskill America.

As one example, Skylab Learning is a startup that has developed several new gaming apps with "snackable" (five- to 10-minute) units that teach vocabulary tailored to workers in the food service industry. The games work on laptops, tablets, and mobile phones. The workers served by the program generally work in low-wage occupations as food service workers, retail employees, and home health care employees. A 2013 evaluation pilot in public libraries in Boston and San Francisco, and in BJ's Wholesale Clubs in New York and Florida, found that 50 percent of participants improved their English language skills by at least one level, as measured by national ESL testing benchmarks, and that the gains occurred over 10-12 weeks, suggesting a more efficient learning experience than longer instructional programs.

The Administration will work closely with innovators, employers, training organizations, and state and local officials across the country to identify and spur the promotion of the most promising tools and technologies to dramatically increase the upskilling opportunity for American workers and employers:

Launching a $25 million Online Skills Academy. An online skills academy will offer open online courses of study, using technology to create high-quality, free or low-cost pathways to degrees, certificates, and other employer-recognized credentials. These pathways will help students prepare for in-demand careers. Courses will be free for all to access, although limited costs may be incurred for students seeking college credit that can be counted toward a degree. Leveraging existing models, the investments will help students earn credentials online through participating accredited institutions, and expand the open access to curriculum designed to speed the time to credit and completion. Other providers can use and augment the open content to provide in-person or other wrap-around services and offer their own degrees or certificates. The online skills academy will leverage the burgeoning marketplace of free and open-licensed learning resources, including content developed through the TAACCCT grant program accessible through DOL's online repository, to ensure that workers can get the education and training they need to advance their careers, particularly in key areas of the economy. The Department of Labor will provide funding to launch the academy through a grant competition in 2015.

To launch the online skills academy, DOL will competitively award $25 million in funds to a consortium to develop career pathways leading to industry-recognized credentials, certificates, and degrees in in-demand fields on an open learning platform. Each pathway would include elements such as competencies recognized by industry and academia; learning resources; high-quality assessment tools; and technology that allows for continuous course improvement. Applicants would be required to demonstrate how their models will be financially sustainable and leverage additional funding from other public and private sources.

Job Skills Innovation Nationwide Prize Competition. Jobs Madness is a national prize competition to bring forward and test radical innovations to upskill workers for higher-wage employment, build accelerated pathways to employment in high-demand sectors, and other innovative technologies outside of the traditional education to employment pathway. Announced today, this national prize competition is run by Innovate & Educate in partnership with the Hope Street Group, CompTIA, the Rockefeller Foundation, the Wadhwani Foundation, Burning Glass Technologies, and STEMconnector.

New Map for Job Seekers to See Where there are Open Jobs. Following the White House Data Jam for Job Seekers, Glassdoor has published a new map for job seekers to see where there are open jobs county-by-county across the country. Recognizing the rising number of dual-earner families, the platform will also enable job seekers to view job density for two jobs at the same time, so a use could better understand where the open jobs are for her or his spouse. Finally, by using their existing resume bank, Glassdoor has determined likely career paths: for example, what percentage of warehouse workers went on to become truck drivers.

Developing New Tool for Job-Relevant and Personalized Career Guidance. Today, Apploi is announcing a commitment to use real-time data about local employer needs to develop a new tool that shows job seekers where the greatest job demand is geographically and by sector, as well as personalized recommendations about what education and training is needed for those positions, primarily focused on jobs in the retail, services, leisure, entertainment, and hospitality industries. In addition, job seekers will be able to learn from their job search by receiving personalized feedback based on their skills, interests, and local job needs. Finally, these search tools will illustrate the possibility for upward mobility and career trajectories, which start with entry-level positions, what training and work experience is necessary to get to the next level, and the best route for such advancement.

3.3 The Tech Workforce: Creating On-Ramps to Fill America's Highest-Demand Jobs

Job opportunities that require information technology (IT) skills are being created in almost every industry, resulting in hundreds of thousands of unfilled positions.[53] IT jobs in fields like cybersecurity, network administration, coding, and data analytics offer pathways to middle-class careers. The lack of IT talent hurts the bottom line of firms whose job openings go unfilled, leaves money on the table for low-wage workers who could substantially improve their earnings with a short-term investment in IT training, and costs the American economy in terms of lost wages and productivity.

Closing the gap between the supply and demand of Americans with IT skills will not be easy and there are no simple solutions, but communities across the country are making progress. Using increased access to specific information about local employer IT demand and the skills required in a constantly evolving IT sector, and forming strong partnerships between the private sector, education

---

[53] CEB TalentNeuron research and analysis, crawling of public profiles, skill predictor algorithms, CEB TalentNeuron Skill Taxonomy & SME Interviews. CEB, 2013.

and training providers, and local leadership, some cities and states are spurring the growth of new models of fast, cost-effective training that allows workers to learn new skills in accelerated programs. Others can emulate these emerging successes. Cybersecurity skills are a particularly pressing need.

Sizing the Need and Opportunity

The Bureau of Labor Statistics projects that between 2012 and 2022, 1.3 million jobs will need to be filled for computer occupations and information systems managers, but the clear message from the private sector is that without serious growth in the number of people with information technology (IT) skills, it is unlikely that American workers will meet that demand.[54]

Source: CEB

Recent analysis from CEB gives a more detailed understanding of metro area labor markets, providing information on supply and demand of talent for specific IT skills. In Philadelphia, for example, in 2013 there were 12,000 IT job opportunities that went unfilled due to a lack of available talent. A closer, skill-level analysis reveals a need for nearly 1,000 developers proficient in Java and 1,110 who possess .NET skills.

IT jobs offer opportunity for American workers across the country. After California, states with the largest number of IT job opportunities include Texas, Georgia, and Illinois. Recent data on the IT job market show that Pennsylvania, Illinois, Oklahoma, and Alabama had the highest demand for IT workers relative to supply. In 2007, 52 percent of software job postings were clustered in just 10 metropolitan areas nationwide, but by 2012 that number had dropped to 45 percent, due largely to demand expanding throughout the country. All signs point to this trend continuing for the foreseeable future.[55]

---

[54] Bureau of Labor Statistics Occupational Employment Projections based on new jobs and replacement need for computer occupations and information systems managers.
[55] "Software Is Everywhere: Growth in Software Jobs," *Burning Glass Technologies*, (July 2013).

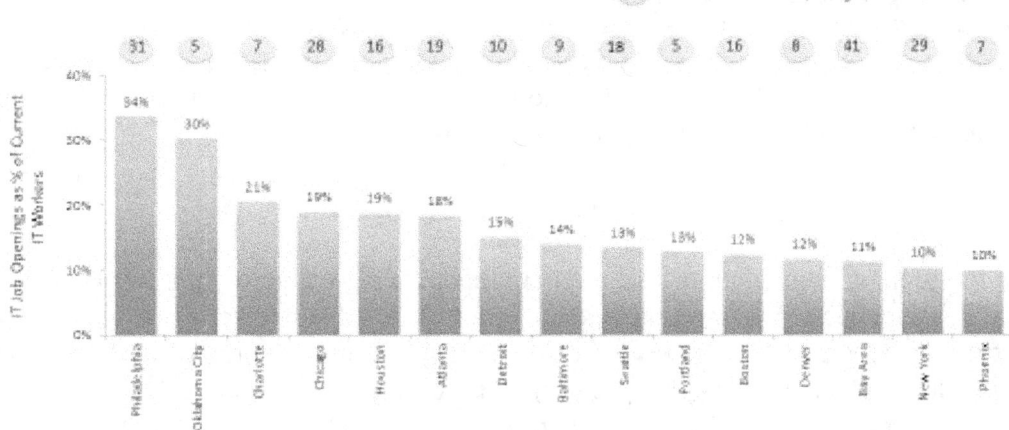

15 U.S. Cities with greater than 10% more Employer IT Job Demand than IT Worker Supply
Local IT Job Openings as % of Current IT Workers, 2013

*These metropolitan areas were selected based on a "material" supply shortage". Material defined as greater than or equal to 10% IT job openings as a percentage of total workforce.
*Metropolitan areas, including cities and surrounding suburbs
SOURCE: CEB

Turning to the sector view, the need for IT workers spans all sectors of the economy, and non-IT industries currently employ two-thirds of private sector IT workers.[56] IT workers in jobs exist in a broad range of industry sectors, with manufacturing being the second largest. The industries experiencing the most rapid growth in IT jobs are outside of the IT sector – the demand for IT workers in retail and health care sectors nearly doubled in 2012 alone.[57]

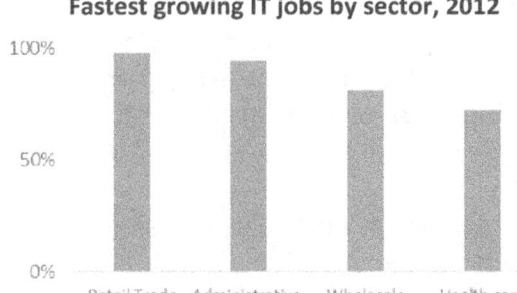

Fastest growing IT jobs by sector, 2012

SOURCE: Burning Glass Technologies

There is also an opportunity to increase the diversity of the IT workforce, with several major employers recognizing the need to take important steps to improve diversity.[58] BLS estimates that 26 percent of workers in computer and mathematical occupations are female, while African-Americans constitute 8 percent and Hispanics constitute 6 percent of this workforce.[59] Each group is underrepresented, offering substantial room to widen the IT talent pipeline.

These issues persist not only in IT, but across the entire STEM talent pool, where women and minorities "now constitute approximately 70 percent of college students while being underrepresented among students who receive undergraduate STEM degrees (approximately 45 percent)."[60]

---

[56] CEB TalentNeuron research and analysis, crawling of public profiles, skill predictor algorithms, CEB TalentNeuron Skill Taxonomy & SME Interviews. CEB, 2013. Unpublsihed
[57] "Software Is Everywhere: Growth in Software Jobs," *Burning Glass Technologies* (July 2013).
[58] "Getting to work on diversity at Google," *Google Official Blog* (May 2014).
[59] "Current Population Survey," *Bureau of Labor Statistics*.
[60] "Engage to Excel: Producing One Million Additional College Graduates with Degrees in Science, Technology, Engineering and Mathematics," *President's Council of Advisors on Science and Technology (PCAST)* (February 2012).

In 2012, the President's Council of Advisors on Science and Technology (PCAST) issued a report demonstrating that the United States needs one million additional STEM college graduates over a decade in order fill critical job openings in science, technology, engineering, and math (STEM) and to continue to reap the economic and social benefits America's leadership in innovation provides. This is an important goal, but given high demand for IT professionals, there are also opportunities to leverage coding boot camps, MOOCs, certification programs, and community colleges to upskill workers in addition to traditional four-year STEM degrees.

Leading IT Job Demand Example: Cybersecurity

Jobs in the burgeoning cybersecurity field are in particularly high demand due to ever-increasing reports of data breaches at major retailers, distributed denial of service attacks on banks, and other malicious cyber incidents. Cybersecurity job postings currently account for 10 percent of all IT job postings, and demand for cybersecurity professionals continues to increase. Cybersecurity job postings grew 74 percent from 2007 to 2013, twice the rate compared to overall IT job market.[61]

Cybersecurity jobs are particularly hard to fill. According to Burning Glass, cybersecurity job postings took 24 percent longer to fill than IT job postings in 2013, and 36 percent longer to fill than all job postings. The supply constraints on cybersecurity jobs means that these professionals command higher salaries: on average, cybersecurity salaries are $15,000 more than the average IT job salary. As with all IT jobs, cybersecurity will provide new opportunities for middle-class jobs for Americans across the country, from all educational backgrounds, and skill levels. The vast majority of cybersecurity jobs – nearly 80 percent – will be in the private sector, rather than in government.[62] Professional services, manufacturing, and finance are currently the leading industries for cybersecurity jobs, but other industries are growing quickly. Burning Glass estimates that industries with the greatest growth in cybersecurity job postings in recent years are retail trade (94 percent growth in job postings from 2010 to 2013), finance and insurance (89 percent growth), and health care (73 percent growth).

Cybersecurity jobs are in demand across industries and geographies, including cities outside of traditional technology hubs: the cities with the fastest growth in cybersecurity job postings in 2013 were Atlanta, Denver, Austin, and Charlotte. Moreover, cybersecurity jobs offer opportunities for those without four-year college degrees. There were nearly 34,000 job postings for cybersecurity jobs in 2013 that did *not* require a bachelor's degree. Cybersecurity jobs are particularly amenable to certification and credentialing programs: 51 percent of all cybersecurity positions request an industry-recognized certification (such as CISSP, CISA, or Security+), compared with 14 percent of IT job postings generally.[84]

Seizing the Opportunity

Closing the gap between the growing demand and the supply of IT-skilled workers cannot be achieved through any single program, initiative, or degree. That being said, preparing Americans to join the tech workforce may be more straightforward and addressable than many other challenges in

---

[61] "Job Market Intelligence: Report on the Growth of Cybersecurity Jobs," *Burning Glass Technologies* (March 2014).
[62] "Global Information Security Workforce Study," *Booz Allen Hamilton* (2013).

the employment space. First, because of the expanding number of employers that are clearly signaling what skills and credentials they will hire to; second, a growth in innovative models for accelerated training; and lastly, partnerships between the private sector, education and training providers, and state and local governments supported by granular, local-level data. The skills that workers need to become job-ready tend to be relatively common across employers, well-documented, and measureable. For instance, the top eight skills needed for IT jobs cover 43 percent of all IT jobs in the United States,[63] and many of these skills can be successfully taught and tested online. Employers are also increasingly accepting competency-based credentials, not just formal academic credentials, in making hiring decisions. Combined with technical certification and testing, credentials provide flexible alternatives to those seeking to retrain in a new field, gain a new skill, or enhance their earning potential for an IT position. This model can save employers time in searching for qualified candidates and save candidates money compared to more expensive traditional degree programs. At the same time, it opens up markets for training providers of all kinds armed with clarity about what skills they should be teaching students to increase job placement rates.

There have also been exciting advances in "accelerated training," a reimagined, competency-based approach to developing technical skills that might otherwise take years of practical experience or expensive four-year degrees to master (see box below).

Advances in Accelerated Training for IT Skills

Defense Advanced Research Projects Agency (DARPA)

One pilot, funded by the Defense Advanced Research Projects Agency (DARPA), trained Navy recruits and unemployed veterans with no previous technical experience to perform at or above the competency level of a 10-year expert with only 16 weeks of intensive training.

Per Scholas

Accelerated training has also been successful at providing entry-level skills that put people on the first rung of the career ladder. Per Scholas, a free, 12-15 week technology job training program has trained more than 4,500 un- and underemployed adults since 1998, has a 77 percent job placement rate.

Finally, opportunities to build upon and expand successful partnerships between local and federal government, and the public and private sector, are substantial and increasingly important. For example, in Cincinnati, Partners for Competitive Workforce (PCW) has facilitated strong partnerships between the CIO Roundtable (25 CIOs responsible for over 6,000 local IT jobs), the Chamber of Commerce, and a range of innovative training opportunities from mid-level career re-training to entry-level support role training. To take another example, the Business-Higher Education Forum (BHEF), a membership organization of Fortune 500 CEOs and college presidents, works to align college and community college curricula with in-demand skills. It has led workforce development projects focused on cybersecurity and IT education, in which universities and community colleges such as California Polytechnic State University and Miami Dade College partner with businesses such as Northrop Grumman, Raytheon, and NextEra Energy to establish undergraduate cybersecurity and IT programs that train for in-demand skills. When it comes to partnerships, the Administration can play an essential convening role, highlighting best practices and new models, setting the tone for mayors

---

[63] CEB TalentNeuron research and analysis, crawling of public profiles, skill predictor algorithms, CEB TalentNeuron Skill Taxonomy & SME Interviews. CEB, 2013.Unpublished

and governors to take up the issue locally, engaging corporate leaders and small business, and increasing communication between a variety of education and training institutions to meet demands across sectors.

Creating more on-ramps to join the tech workforce is a significant lever to increase access to the middle class and ensure long-term global competitiveness for American companies. The Administration, alongside the public and private sector and state and local governments, can seize the opportunity to make a substantial difference in employment and wage growth nationwide. To begin addressing the opportunity to close the gap between employer needs and a workforce ready to fill them, the Administration will take the following actions in partnership with the private sector:

National Initiative for Cybersecurity Education (NICE) to Increase Access to Cybersecurity Education and Training. NICE, which is designed to improve cybersecurity education from K-12 to post-graduate schools in the United States, is taking new actions to expand the number of individuals who are prepared for in-demand cybersecurity jobs. NICE aims to expand pathways to cyber skills and jobs by developing an interactive U.S. map that shows where cybersecurity job openings exist while identifying for applicants the skills the jobs require and the training programs available to applicants seeking each job. NICE is also developing a plan to expand pathways to cybersecurity skills and jobs by expanding the list of high-quality cyber training programs certified by the Department of Homeland Security and the National Security Agency, particularly in community colleges.

Expanding Innovative Coding Bootcamps. Three cities – Kansas City, Missouri; Louisville, Kentucky; and Minneapolis, Minnesota – together with the Wadhwani Foundation, are creating new public-private partnerships, working closely with local IT employers and city leaders to attract coding bootcamps. Each will quantify employer demand for IT positions and specific skills necessary to fill those jobs, and will identify funding immediately available to provide tuition support. The Wadhwani Foundation will provide support to document and evaluate these efforts as they move forward.

Department of Veterans Affairs Accelerated Learning Competition. To ensure that veterans can take full advantage of innovative learning models, the Department of Veterans Affairs will sponsor a $10 million competition to identify leading practices among alternative learning models and will evaluate the employment outcomes of accelerated learning programs (ALPs) for post-9/11 veterans. The competition will be a multi-staged event leading to direct funding of veteran participation in IT-centric ALPs, including coding bootcamps. This two-year demonstration project will start in FY 2015, with the help of funding through the VA Center for Innovation, and has the potential to scale to other communities based on demonstrated outcomes and the availability of resources.